Inspiralized

Inspiralized

Inspiring recipes to make with your spiralizer

ALI MAFFUCCI

PHOTOGRAPHS BY EVAN SUNG

EBURY
PRESS

Ebury Press, an imprint of Ebury Publishing,
20 Vauxhall Bridge Road, London, SW1V 2SA

Ebury Press is part of the Penguin Random House group
of companies whose addresses can be found at global.
penguinrandomhouse.com

Penguin
Random House
UK

Copyright © Alissandra Maffucci 2015
Photography © Evan Sung 2015
Alissandra Maffucci has asserted her right to be identified as the
author of this Work in accordance with the Copyright, Designs
and Patents Act 1988

First published by Ebury Press in 2015

This edition published by arrangement with Clarkson Potter/
Publishers, a division of Random House, Inc., a Penguin Random
House Company, New York. All rights reserved.

www.eburypublishing.co.uk

A CIP catalogue record for this book is
available from the British Library

Anglicised by Lee Faber
Design: Ashley Tucker
Photography: Evan Sung
Photograph on page 10:
courtesy of the author
Photograph on page 11:
Nadya Furnari Photography
Photographs on pages 12, 33 and
213: Unique Lapin Photography

ISBN: 9781785031304

Colour origination by BORN Ltd
Printed and bound in Italy by Printer
Trento S.r.l.

Penguin Random House is committed to a
sustainable future for our business, our readers
and our planet. This book is made from Forest
Stewardship Council® certified paper.

FSC
www.fsc.org

MIX
Paper from
responsible sources
FSC® C018179

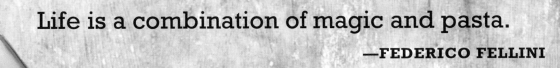

Life is a combination of magic and pasta.

—FEDERICO FELLINI

Some are born with silver spoons in their mouths, some with plastic ones, and some with none. All I know is that my spoon was definitely dripping with tomato-basil sauce.

This book is dedicated to my Italian-American grandparents, who brought love and joy into our family through food. Thank you for making cooking and, most of all, eating so much fun.

Special dedication to:

Mum, for your undying support, love, and faith in me.

Dad, for teaching me to work hard for what I want.

Lu, for inspiring me to start *Inspiralized* and being my daily taste tester. I love you.

My Grandmother Ida, for giving me my thirst for knowledge.

My *Inspiralized* readers: Thanks to your loyal support and following, this cookbook was made possible.

And to all lovers of pasta and carbs. *Salute!*

CONTENTS

If I had a pound for every time my Italian grand-parents said, 'We're on a diet – we're giving up pasta, wine, and cheese', I wouldn't be here writing this book. I'd be living on an island with my riches.

Sunday-night dinners at the home of my father's parents were always quite the scene. My sweet grandmother – a woman who proudly donned her Sunday best for Mass and washed my mouth out with soap for saying 'pee' instead of 'tinkle' – would be burning something in the oven and scuffling about the kitchen with a spoon in her hand, dripping sauce on the tiled floors. But despite the chaos, Pops, with his big gold pinky ring, strong nose, and all-consuming love of the motherland, always managed to prepare flawless meatballs or the perfect pesto.

Cooking was always the main event. The party didn't start when everyone arrived for dinner; it started when the first *glug* of olive oil hit the pan, signalling the beginning of a beautiful, delicious Italian meal. We were all pulled in not only by the smell of a fresh marinara simmering but also by the clinks of wine glasses filled with full-bodied reds and sounds of Pops's favourite Frank Sinatra album (if you could hear the songs over his own renditions). The sight of Pops twirling my grandmother around to 'That's Amore' is unforgettable.

Eating was another spectacle. My father would fight anyone for the last piece of bread to dip in the sauce left on his plate – God forbid we didn't savour every last drop. The wine flowed, and my grandmother constantly got up to bring something else to the table, whether olive oil, more bread, or freshly grated Parmesan. Despite conversations that could be either negative or positive, the mood was always jovial, simply because we were *eating*. We gorged ourselves on pasta, meats, wine, and cheese nearly to the point of discomfort – yet we never missed dessert. And that was always an assortment of Italian pastries from a *molto bene* bakery – *biscotti*, *sfogliatelle*, *pignoli*. My personal favourite was *cannoli* and *Sambuca*, the little espresso beans floating in that sweet anise-flavoured liqueur paired with decadent ricotta-filled pastry. By the time we left my grandparents we had eaten our weight in carbohydrates, but we were happy. My grandmother and Pops would walk us out the front door and wait to wave good-bye as we drove out the driveway. Everyone was already excited for the next Sunday.

When I had the opportunity to spend a university term studying abroad, I of course went to Italy. I treated every day as if it were Sunday night dinner at my grandparents'. I devoured pizzas, polished off aromatic Chiantis, ripped through *caprese* salads, slurped up giant portions of pasta bolognese, and dipped fresh semolina bread into whatever I could get my hands on. I might as well have just slurped olive oil straight from the bottle. When I returned home, I had to face the consequences of my indulgences: high numbers on the scale. I had put on an embarassing 9kg during my indulgent European term, bringing my grand total weight gain to 23kg since first year. When I saw that number, I knew something had to change.

I gave myself some leniency, as I was suffering withdrawal from *la dolce vita*, after all. Then my friend Sarah gave me a book on – are you sitting down? – veganism. Despite fear of a painful good-bye to sausage, mozzarella, thick pestos, meatballs, and white pastas and breads, I was quickly sold on the promises of slender arms and skinny thighs. In August 2008, I began a two-year stint as a vegan and it worked: I lost 27kg and obtained the arms and thighs of my dreams. But, there was one big problem: Sunday night dinners at my grandparents' were different – and not in a good way. Telling my family I was a vegan was like telling them I was moving to the most desolate corner of the world. Wholegrain pasta and multigrain bread just weren't part of Pops's vocabulary. Luckily, my grandparents' unconditional love prevailed, and they made extra dishes for me: more vegetables, wholemeal spaghetti, and pasta fagioli. It just wasn't the same, though.

As a result of adopting veganism, I learned how to cook creatively and healthfully, discovered new types of food, and became empowered by my knowledge of fresh, clean eating and its immense health benefits. As an Italian-American and lover of pastas and savoury foods, I still struggled with portion

control – until my mother introduced me to the spiralizer. After that, my life changed.

So, how did it all start?

My mother is a Type 1 diabetic. This type of diabetes, which often begins in childhood, is known as insulin-dependent diabetes because the pancreas produces little or no insulin, a hormone that normally converts glucose (sugar) into energy. If not managed properly, this chronic diabetes can cause serious health problems, such as kidney failure, blindness, nerve damage, fatal heart disease, and stroke. Although there are many causes for diabetes, my mother initially developed gestational diabetes, becoming diabetic while pregnant. In 2012, when I was living in Hoboken, New Jersey, she started seeing a health coach who suggested she try raw veganism, a diet that excludes not only all animal products but also foods cooked above a temperature of about 48°C/118°F.

A few weeks later, on holiday in Florida, she researched raw vegan restaurants and found one nearby. She figured she would try out restaurant-quality raw food before committing to the lifestyle. She ordered a 'Dragon Bowl', which listed courgette noodles as one of its ingredients. My mother was impressed and amazed by it – so much so that she told me about the dish right away. She wanted to recreate those courgette noodles at home, but she didn't know how.

A few months later, in New York City, we went to a raw organic restaurant called Pure Food and Wine. We had an incredible meal,

so my mother was committed to eating more vegan and plant-based foods. She bought the restaurant's cookery book, and that's when she discovered the spiralizer. One of the recipes in the book was for courgette noodles.

My mother insisted I should try these noodles, but I was incredulous: how could a vegetable noodle taste like pasta, especially to someone who had grown up eating so much pasta? Then, one Sunday evening she made me a dish with them. I was floored. I was expecting something either crunchy and raw or mushy and overcooked, but what I tasted was the same lovely consistency of *al dente* pasta. Honestly, if my eyes had been closed, I would have thought she had served me real spaghetti!

Always looking for new ways to eat healthfully, I was captivated. Most importantly, I regretted not having tried it sooner. I apologized for being so stubborn, and I thanked my mother. She sent me home with her spiralizer and bought another for herself.

I counted the hours at work the next day, eager to go home and make courgette noodles for my dinner that night. I decided to make a tomato-basil pasta with cannellini beans, roasted artichokes, and prawns. In just minutes, I had a pasta dish that was low-calorie, low-carb, and nutritious. And it seemed to come so naturally. Although my mother had presented the courgette noodles as a spaghetti replacement, I saw that they had greater potential. As soon as I started turning the handle of my spiralizer, recipe ideas began filling my head.

Lu, my boyfriend at the time, had no idea what I was doing, of course. He was just hungry, as usual. When the meal was ready, I tasted the dish and knew I had something special. Lu took his first bite, threw his head back, and roared, 'Mmmm!'

'I know, right?' I said excitedly.

Immediately, he responded, 'How come everyone doesn't know about this?'

For the next three months, all I could do was think about spiralizing. If I went to a coffee shop on the weekend, I'd bring my laptop to write recipes, and I left wanting to test them that evening. I felt this great urge to *create*. After years of working in static corporate environments, I finally had an outlet: spiralizing had inspired me! Simply put, I was *Inspiralized*, and I wanted to Inspiralize others.

The more I cooked spiralized meals, the more convinced I became of their potential. I started posting pictures of my spiralized dinners on my social media channels, and my friends commented back, asking for the recipes. When I told them the noodles were made with a spiralizer, they bought their own to get started. I was creating buzz in my own social circle, so I knew the idea would catch on just as quickly with the rest of the world.

I was especially happy to tell everyone on low-carb diets that pasta and noodle bowls could be enjoyed again, and not just on 'cheat day'. Like them, I was tired of green juices and boring lean proteins and veggies for dinner. I also couldn't find truly diet-friendly food that tasted great. But now I had the key to that castle!

When I searched online for 'spiralized recipes', everything that turned up was raw, vegan, or both. The only recipes I could find stuck to three basic veggies: carrots, cucumbers, and courgettes. No one was capturing the true power of the spiralizer.

Finally, in June 2013, after mustering up the necessary courage, I walked into my boss's office and quit my job. Then I rushed home, bright-eyed and bushy-tailed, and purchased the domain name Inspiralized.com. That next morning, I walked into a coffee shop across the street, opened up my laptop, and without a clue as to how to start a blog, I wrote my first post and began drafting a business plan.

In order to create and test recipes that did not exclude any types of eaters, I went from vegan to pescatarian to omnivore again.

Re-introducing these favourite foods to my diet was welcomed, not feared. I took a culinary journey that allowed me to manage my waistline as I adapted all my food knowledge to this new spiralized way of cooking. My body has slimmed down, my skin glows, and I have more energy than ever before.

Most important? Sunday dinners at my grandparents' house are again satisfying and delicious.

GETTING INSPIRALIZED

Inspiralized is what your meal and *you* become – a healthy and inspired version of the original! When you work vegetable noodles and vegetable rice into your diet, you'll start to notice the effects almost instantly: glowing skin, better digestion, more energy, and overall dietary satisfaction. You will no longer crave the heavy carbs, sugars, or processed foods. Your body will be so satisfied and so well nourished that you'll forget about 'real' pasta and noodles and 'real' rice, and you'll yearn for more lean, whole, and clean foods. Most importantly, you'll want to invent your own recipes, whether that means adapting the classics and your favourites or experimenting with new ideas. You'll find yourself eager to get home and Inspiralize.

The Health Benefits

These days, *healthy* is a relative and confusing term. We've lost the concept of what's truly healthy; we place labels on strict diets that we follow instead of learning what works best for our own bodies. Of course, for some of us, strict guidelines can help keep a weight-loss journey on track or help manage an illness. Regardless of your food outlook, you'll be hard-pressed to find a dietary lifestyle that doesn't advocate eating more vegetables.

When you add more vegetables to your diet, the health benefits are immense. They include:

HIGHER INTAKE OF DIETARY FIBRE: The fibre in vegetables helps reduce blood cholesterol levels and therefore may lower the risk of heart disease. Dietary fibre also helps provide a feeling of fullness with fewer calories, which promotes overall weight loss and health maintenance.

MORE NUTRIENT DENSITY: Simply put, vegetables have tons of nutrients. Vitamins A and C help keep your skin healthy and your immune system strong, respectively; potassium and folate help your muscles function and your body to build cells, respectively. Overall, these nutrients keep your body running optimally and keep you feeling more energized.

DISEASE PREVENTION: Many studies prove that a diet rich in veggies and fruits slows the absorption of sugar into your bloodstream, lowering the risk of diabetes. Plus, a veggie- and fruit-rich diet prevents fatty substances from sticking to blood vessel walls, helping defend against heart disease.

Imagine if you ate a big bowl of wheat pasta, but didn't feel uncomfortable or lethargic afterwards; instead of needing to lie down, you felt like going dancing or taking a walk with your dinner date. Instead of feeling guilty for indulging, you felt that you were doing something positive for your body. That's what it will be like if you eat a bowl of vegetable noodles – same great taste, but with a much better feeling afterwards.

Now, I'm not suggesting that you never again eat a bowl of regular pasta or rice. Carbohydrates are a crucial part of a healthy, balanced diet, and they should be eaten in their recommended daily amounts. However, they should be consumed in a whole, unprocessed form so you can best absorb their health benefits. Adding spiralized sweet potatoes to a meal, for example, is an effective way to obtain those clean carbohydrates. But if you're at a restaurant and feel like having a bowl of spaghetti bolognese, go for it – everything in moderation, always.

Nutritional Information: Pasta Noodles vs. Vegetable Noodles

Now, let's get to the facts and figures of it all. Looking at a nutritional comparison of the most commonly spiralized vegetables and regular wheat pasta reveals the stark differences. The chart below shows a proper

Pasta Noodles vs. Vegetable Noodles

	SERVING SIZE	CALORIES	CARBS	PROTEIN	FAT
Wheat spaghetti	140g	221	43g	8g	1.3g
Carrot	190g	77.9	19g	1.7g	0.4g
Cucumber	398g	30.4	6.84g	1.14g	0.19g
Beetroot	150g	64.5	15g	2.4g	0.3g
Butternut squash	180g	81	21.6g	1.8g	0.18g
Kohlrabi	385g	71.82	15.96g	4.5g	0.27g
Courgette	245g	41.7	7.6g	2.9g	0.7g

serving of vegetable noodles and the recommended serving of wheat pasta, as indicated in the box. When you eat a pasta dish at a restaurant, the quantity is often double or triple that recommended serving!

All of the serving sizes for the vegetable pastas are based on a plentiful bowl of raw noodles. If cooked, they yield 140g–398g of vegetable noodles. Keep in mind that there are no guidelines for vegetable pasta serving sizes. These are just best practices that have been suggested, tested, and 'approved' by me.

Of course, with spiralizing, you can vary and combine vegetables to obtain varied amounts of vitamins and minerals; that is, you can build meals based on your own dietary needs, which isn't possible with regular pasta and noodles. For example, those who suffer from an iron deficiency could substitute spiralized potatoes and broccoli, both high in iron. Add spinach and some beans, and you'll pack in more than enough iron in one delicious meal. Can regular pasta do that?

Daily Vegetable Intake

We're always being told to eat our vegetables. Well, if you're not a veggie lover, I have good news. By eating vegetable noodles or vegetable rice, you easily take in your daily recommended amount of veggies without it tasting like you are. Instead of begrudgingly puréeing the vegetable into a smoothie or eating it in a boring side salad, you can build it into a big, satisfying dish. In fact, when you toss a bowl of courgette or butternut squash noodles with a creamy basil pesto, you'll be

getting your daily recommended amount of vegetables while feeling you're eating a decadent bowl of spaghetti. For example, a woman in her forties should consume 250g of vegetables per day. With just one bowl of courgette noodles, she has achieved that – without having to force down a green juice or some steamed broccoli.

In short, spiralized vegetables can be 'disguised' as pasta, noodles, and rice, transforming them into popular forms. Some unexpected guises include:

IN A FRITTATA (Chorizo and Avocado Courgette Frittata, page 36)

IN A SOUP (Chicken Carrot Noodle Soup, page 76)

IN NACHOS (Spicy Butternut Squash Nachos, page 60)

IN SUSHI (Beetroot Rice Nori Rolls, page 106)

IN A DESSERT (Pecan and Carrot Almond Butter Bars, page 194)

These are just a few of the many creative capabilities and versatilities of spiralized vegetables – in fact, this book is full of them! You'll quickly find what works best for you.

Family and Child-Friendly Cooking

So many parents complain, 'I can't get my kids to eat vegetables!' Well, what child doesn't love spaghetti? Whether eating it messily with their hands at age 1 or with a fork at age 4, most kids love noodles. Make a simple bowl of courgette noodles with tomato sauce and watch your toddler dig in – he or she will never know it's the 'yucky' green stuff. If spaghetti doesn't do the trick, you can make elbow macaroni carrot noodles and top them with a light cheese sauce (see page 131). When you master the spiralized bun (see page 26), you'll be able to create sandwiches out of heart-healthy veggies such as sweet potatoes. For an after-school snack, fit in a fruit-and-vegetable double whammy with the Apple-Potato Cheese Bun (page 119). You can also nurse your child back to health with Chicken Carrot Noodle Soup (page 76) using carrots instead of pasta, thereby providing beta-carotene, a powerful phytonutrient that boosts the immune system's production of infection-fighting natural cells. But that'll be our little secret.

Even better, toddlers and young kids love to get in on spiralizing. Who wouldn't have fun seeing a vegetable magically turn into noodles? There's no better way to teach your children healthy eating habits than to have them help you in the kitchen. Inadvertently, your children will learn that vegetables are fun.

Spiralized cooking is family-friendly because it's fast. When you're juggling football practice, dance recitals, homework, and more, you don't have much time left for cooking nutritious meals. But it takes only about 30 seconds to spiralize a courgette and only 2–3 minutes to cook the noodles to *al dente* (versus 5 minutes to boil water and 10–15 minutes to cook wheat pasta). To really save time, you can spiralize your vegetable noodles ahead. For information on preparing vegetable noodles in advance, see the tips on pages 28–29.

READY, SET, SPIRALIZE!

So, how does it work, exactly? Let's get into everything you need to know to start spiralizing in your own kitchen.

The What

One of the best things about spiralizing is that it introduces you to new vegetables. Eventually, you'll be in the supermarket asking yourself, 'Can I spiralize that?' Maybe you'll find something you've never tasted before – or even something you hadn't heard of until then. With these guidelines, you'll know straight away.

The vegetable or fruit must be solid, with no tough stone, seedy interior, or hollow core. The only exception here is butternut squash, whose bulbous bottom has a seedy centre. Prior to spiralizing, just chop that part off – the rest of the vegetable fits the bill.

The vegetable must be at least 4cm in diameter for optimal spiralizing. If the vegetable is any smaller, it will be tough to get perfect pasta-like spirals; instead, you'll have half-moon shapes. The larger the diameter, the better.

The vegetable or fruit must be at least 4cm in length. While the vegetable won't yield many noodles this long, that's the shortest length you should use; otherwise, the vegetable will be mostly wasted.

The vegetable or fruit cannot be soft or juicy inside. The outer skin should be tough, unless you're peeling it. If you are peeling the skin, then the interior should be dense and firm. If you try spiralizing a juicy pineapple, for example, the fruit will fall apart.

There is one major exception to all these rules: aubergine. Because of its soft flesh and tiny seeds, it won't work well. When you load the aubergine in, you'll notice immediately upon cranking the handle that it resists the movement. Its flesh will be chopped, and any noodles that do materialize will be soft and break with a firm pinch. A very large aubergine yields only about 125g of noodles – a big waste. I don't recommend spiralizing aubergine, and I have not included it in this cookbook.

So what *does* work? Depending on which part of the world you live in, you'll find some fruits or veggies unavailable locally or you may have some that other parts of the country do not have. If you don't see a familiar vegetable or fruit on the following list, refer to the above guidelines to determine if it can be spiralized.

These are my favourite vegetables for spiralizing, and they are the basis for recipes in this book:

Apple	Parsnip
Beetroot	Pear
Broccoli (stems only)	Plantain
Butternut squash	Radish
Cabbage	Swede
Carrot	Sweet potato (and yam)
Celeriac	
Courgette	Turnip
Kohlrabi	White potato
Onion	

When choosing a vegetable or fruit, consider its texture, colour, nutritional balance, and, of course, flavour. For information regarding best uses, preparations, cooking methods, serving sizes, nutritional values, and health benefits of each specific vegetable and fruit on this list, see pages 208–217.

The How

We know *why* incorporating spiralized vegetables into our diets is beneficial, and we know *what* we can and cannot spiralize . . . but how do we actually *do* it?

Prepping

Prior to spiralizing, you must always prepare your vegetable or fruit. If the skin of whatever you are using is inedible, or if you prefer not to eat it, peel it off. However, do keep in mind that many important vitamins and nutrients in vegetables and fruits are found in the skin.

Next, be sure the ends of the fruit or vegetable are as even and flat as possible. If they are not flat (say, rounded, as for a beetroot), you can just slice off a small piece to flatten the ends.

If you are finding that a particular vegetable does not spiralize easily, it could be because there is not enough surface area for the spiralizer to grip on to. Remember, you're looking for a minimum of 4cm in diameter. Also, in an effort to get the vegetable as straight as possible and with flat ends, you may need to trim off edible parts of the vegetable or fruit; that can be frustrating, but save those trimmings for future cooking, or just snack along the way!

You also may want to cut some long vegetables in half crossways to give yourself better leverage with the spiralizer. Generally, anything longer than 15cm should be halved. This rule almost always applies to butternut squash, but also to some bigger sweet potatoes, courgettes, and cucumbers.

Choosing Your Blade

When you've prepped your vegetable, it's ready to be spiralized. You select the blade depending on what recipe you're making and what type of noodles it requires. Most spiralizers on the market today come with three or four blades. The recipes in this book indicate whether to use the A, B, C, or D blade. Here are descriptions to help you figure out which blades I'm indicating:

BLADE A: Yields thin, ribboned noodles similar to pappardelle.

BLADE B: Yields noodles similar to fettuccine.

BLADE C: Yields noodles similar to linguine and spaghetti.

BLADE D: Yields the thinnest noodles, similar to angel hair. (This blade should be used on skinnier vegetables. It can also be used interchangeably with blade C.)

BLADE A

BLADE B

BLADE C

My spiralizer uses these lettered labels on the blade-changing knobs, but if yours is another brand, you'll want to check its manual so you know which blade makes which noodle. Most blades have either comb-like teeth or triangle-shaped spokes. The smaller the distance between the teeth or the smaller the triangular spokes, the thinner the noodle produced. If the blade doesn't have *any* teeth or triangular spokes, then it's always blade A.

If you don't have a spiralizer yet, you can still make spaghetti-like strands using a julienne peeler or mandoline. These won't yield long, spiral-like noodles, but they are a great way to start enjoying vegetable pasta!

Cooking with Spiralized Rice

	YIELDS (G)	RAW OR COOKED	COOK TIME (MINUTES)
Beetroot	270	Both	10
Butternut squash	Up to 400	Cooked	10–15
Carrots	360	Raw	5–10
Celeriac	Up to 400	Both	10–15
Courgettes	125–170	Both	2–3
Daikon radish*	300	Both	5–10
Kohlrabi	330	Both	5–10
Plantains	150	Cooked	10–15
Swede	Up to 400	Cooked	10–15
Sweet potatoes	230	Cooked	10–-5
Turnips*	150–200	Both	10
Courgette	1½–2	Both	2–3

*Squeeze out excess moisture after pulsing and prior to cooking.

Beyond the Noodle

When you start spiralizing, you'll most likely begin by making pasta dishes. You'll rejoice in the fact that you're appreciating vegetables in a whole new way – as the superhero, not as the trusty sidekick. But after a while, you will wonder, 'Okay, what's next?' The sky's the limit: you can Inspiralize any meal. It's always fun and is always surprising.

Spiralized Rice

One afternoon I was testing some new cooking methods, and I placed butternut squash noodles into boiling water. Big mistake; the noodles broke apart, practically disintegrating. It was a seemingly failed experiment, until I suddenly realized: it looked just like rice! I ran with it, making Spanish rice with ham and olives, sweet potato fried rice, risotto with peas, and even plantain rice and beans. I quickly realized this technique was just as powerful as making vegetable noodles.

With vegetable rice, you don't need expensive rice cookers, watery boil-in-a-bag grains, or mushy and preservative-laden frozen versions. Instead, in under 5 minutes, you can have a totally unprocessed and nutritious option. This party trick makes it possible to reinvent more of your favourites, typically those indulgent dishes. Burrito bowls, stuffed peppers, risottos, pilafs, casseroles, curries, and paella – you name it. You can make vegetable rice from all vegetables that can be spiralized, except those that have a high water content. The chart opposite shows which vegetables make the best rice, how much they yield, and how to cook them.

There are many ways to cook spiralized rice:

BAKED IN THE OVEN: Vegetable rice works well in casseroles. It can be added raw and then slowly baked until cooked through.

SAUTÉED IN A FRYING PAN: Cook the vegetable rice with your oil of choice, tossing occasionally, and season to your preference.

SIMMERED IN A STOCK OR SAUCE: Add the vegetable rice to a simmering sauce or pour stock over the rice and simmer until cooked.

How to Make Spiralized Rice

Spiralize your vegetable of choice using blade C or blade D. Place the noodles in a food processor and pulse until they look rice-like. For those vegetables that need draining, just squeeze the rice over the sink to rid it of excess moisture before cooking.

Spiralized Buns

My idea for spiralized buns originated during the ramen burger craze in the summer of 2013, in Williamsburg, Brooklyn. At Smorgasburg, an outdoor pop-up food market, hundreds of people were waiting in line for ramen burgers. They are exactly what they sound like: a burger on a bun made from packed ramen noodles. Seeing them, I immediately wanted to create a healthier version – so I did! (See below.)

Vegetable noodle buns are not only gluten-free but also full of nutrients, unlike the typical puffy wheat or potato bun. These buns can be used to sandwich burgers, serve as open-faced sandwiches, or even form the basis for miniature pizzas. Check the chart on this page to see which vegetables are best for use as buns and how many buns can be made with each.

	YIELDS (BUNS)
Large potatoes (all types)	2–3
Large parsnips	1–2
Large swede	6
Large celeriac	3–4
Large plantain	1–2

Let's Get Cooking

I'm not a professionally trained chef, nor have I ever worked in a restaurant kitchen. I have definitely roasted meats too long and whisked eggs backwards, and I can't effortlessly chop garlic. But that's okay. On the whole, there's no right or wrong way to cook. For those of us who love to cook but don't have the means or desire to acquire culinary training,

How to Make Spiralized Buns

Spiralize your vegetable of choice using blade C. Season and then sauté the noodles in a large frying pan. Transfer to a medium bowl, add an egg, and toss to coat. Pack into a ramekin or similar vessel and place aluminium foil or greaseproof paper directly onto the noodles. Press down with your hands or a weighted can, then allow to set for 15 minutes in the fridge. Heat 1 tablespoon olive oil in a large frying pan over a medium heat. When the oil is shimmering, invert the moulded noodle cake into the pan. Sear until the bun is firm and browned on both sides, about 5 minutes.

trial-and-error learning can go a long way. With spiralizing, you really enjoy being in the kitchen because not only is the spiralizing fun and easy, but you're also healthfully transforming your meals in a stunning way!

For a few years now, I've been spiralizing nearly every day, multiple times a day. I've tried to spiralize every conceivable vegetable and fruit, and I've had my share of 'oops' and 'aha!' moments. With my tips and tricks, you should have all the information and forewarnings you need for a seamless experience.

Clean the Spiralizer Regularly

Certain vegetables (beetroot, carrots, sweet potatoes) are brightly coloured and have oils and juices that can easily stain your spiralizer if you're not careful. I suggest buying a round palm brush solely for cleaning the spiralizer. The brush will make it easier to scrub the blades and remove any discolouration before it sets. Use soap and water, and clean just as soon as you finish spiralizing. The blades can be sharp, so the dedicated brush will save you from ruining others.

Avoid a Watery Sauce with Courgette Noodles

The number one e-mail question I get from my readers is, 'Why are my courgette noodles sitting in a pool of liquid?' If you're using a tomato-based sauce, the chances are there will be excess liquid in your pasta bowl. The longer the courgette noodles sit in a sauce like this, the more time they have to release their natural moisture, making the whole dish runny. Well, this is to be expected, since courgettes are 95 per cent water! What's the silver lining? Foods rich in water cleanse your body naturally by providing up to a litre of fluid daily. Since most vegetables are high in fibre and water, they are digested more quickly than other foods, allowing the body to use its energy for detoxifying instead of digesting.

Nevertheless, you can reduce the amount of water that will result. Here are some key tricks:

A 70:30 NOODLE-TO-SAUCE RATIO. Lean more heavily on the noodles – add more noodles or simply use less sauce.

PAT THE VEGETABLES VERY DRY BEFORE COOKING. This is especially important for cucumber noodles. Patting dry with kitchen paper or a tea towel will remove excess moisture that appears when the inside of the vegetable is exposed after spiralizing.

FULLY REDUCE YOUR SAUCE BEFORE ADDING TO YOUR VEGGIE NOODLES. Simmer your sauce until it's thick so there is no excess liquid. Doing so also concentrates the flavours.

ADD FOODS TO YOUR DISH THAT WILL SOAK UP MOISTURE. Stir in beans, cheeses, meats, and wholemeal breadcrumbs. They all absorb liquid, thereby thickening your sauce.

COOK THE NOODLES SEPARATELY AND DRAIN THEM BEFORE ADDING THE SAUCE. If you are not in a rush, and don't mind dirtying extra dishes, cook the noodles briefly with only a little cooking spray in a heated frying pan; allow to drain in a colander, and pat dry. When your sauce is done, pour it over the cooked noodles and then serve.

USE PASTA TONGS TO DRAIN THE NOODLES WHEN SERVING. Never pour out the contents of your frying pan into a bowl to serve. When your pasta is cooked and ready to serve, remove the noodles with pasta tongs, allowing any excess moisture to drip off or remain in the pan.

Cutting the Noodles with Scissors

If you could continuously spiralize a vegetable with no breaks, it would yield one ridiculously long noodle. A reader once sent me a video of her child skipping with a courgette noodle! Long noodles from perfectly straight and uniform vegetables are tough to serve and portion out. To make serving easier, use kitchen scissors to trim the noodles after spiralizing. You can go centimetre by centimetre or just grab a bunch and roughly snip. Either way, you'll get shorter noodles that are easier to divide onto plates and easier to eat. If you forget this step, don't worry, though – you can still do it after they've cooked.

Avoid Half-Moon Noodles

You will notice that the spiralizer slices some of the vegetable into half-moon shapes while you're making the spiral noodles. This happens mostly when the vegetable moves off centre. To avoid this, simply stop and reposition your vegetable or fruit so that it keeps centred on the cylindrical coring blade. With smaller vegetables, you may have to do this repeatedly. Also, be sure the ends of your vegetables are flat. Uneven ends are tough to secure in the spiralizer and will cause the vegetable to dislodge or misalign.

If you end up with a growing pile of half-moons, don't throw them out. Use them in a pasta salad; their neat shape takes nicely to salad dressing and resembles big elbow macaroni pasta.

Store Your Spiralized Veggies in the Fridge or Freezer for Plan-Ahead Meals

Adopting a healthier diet requires staying focused and avoiding temptation. Meal planning, therefore, becomes your best friend. Nothing's worse than looking in your fridge and finding only condiments. When that happens, you are inclined to order a pizza or get 'the usual' at your favourite takeaway.

To avoid such situations, you can store prepared vegetable noodles and vegetable rices in your fridge. *All* vegetable noodles can be prepared in advance and refrigerated or frozen for future use. Just line a glass or plastic container with kitchen paper and seal in an airtight container.

All vegetable noodles keep in the fridge for up to 4 days. After 4 or 5 days, though, they will stiffen and lose their flavour. The following are exceptions to this rule:

CUCUMBERS last only 2 or 3 days in the fridge because of their very high water content.

APPLES, PEARS, AND WHITE POTATOES brown (oxidize) when spiralized, and are thereafter difficult to prep in advance.

Vegetable noodles that freeze well include sweet potatoes, swede, carrots, beetroot, butternut squash, parsnips, celeriac, kohlrabi, and broccoli stems. As they defrost, they will wilt, making them even easier to cook.

You can also save whole leftover spiralized meals in the fridge for a few days. Be aware that if you are using courgette or cucumber noodles, though, excess moisture will slowly be released the longer the leftovers sit in the fridge. When reheating, drain away some liquid first to avoid a soupy sauce. This isn't a problem with other vegetable noodles.

The Inspiralized Kitchen

Certain kitchen tools are helpful for easily whipping up the meals in this book. In order of importance, consider having on hand:

FOOD PROCESSOR: Food processors are not only necessary for making spiralized rice but also are helpful for making clean salad dressings, pasta sauces, and breadcrumbs. No need to buy a giant one that won't fit in your kitchen; I use a 750ml food processor and that size works well.

PASTA TONGS: To properly cook your vegetable noodles, you need tongs to toss them. This tool will also help you serve your finished recipes. I suggest a rubber pair for their gentleness when handling delicate vegetables.

QUALITY CHEF'S KNIFE: Before I started cooking, I never understood why professional chefs were so attached to their knives, but now I get it! Some vegetables are tough to peel and prep for spiralizing, such as celeriac, butternut squash, and swede. Without a quality knife that can easily cut through the flesh, your cooking experience may be less than pleasant.

NON-STICK FRYING PANS: All my recipes require non-stick frying pans, for a simple reason: cooking vegetable pasta in a regular frying pan can be disastrous – the noodles stick, rip, and fall apart. If you don't already have one, start with a large non-stick frying pan, then add to your collection later. I recommend 20cm, 25cm, and 30cm frying pans.

VEGETABLE PEELER: Carrots, beetroot, butternut squash, swede, kohlrabi, celeriac, and plantain must be peeled prior to spiralizing. Other vegetables, such as courgettes, can be peeled for a softer noodle, but doing so is not necessary. Peeling with a knife can be inefficient, difficult, dangerous, and time-consuming. I use two peelers—one with ridges for the very tough-skinned vegetables and one without for softer skins, like courgettes.

ROUND PALM BRUSH: A dedicated brush for cleaning your spiralizer. Refer to page 27 for more details.

Other essential kitchen tools include a spatula, a chopping board, and at least two baking sheets. And other tools that would be helpful, but not completely necessary, are a high-speed blender, a slow cooker, and a griddle pan.

The Inspiralized Pantry

Stocking your pantry with interesting condiments, seasonings, and foods will keep you from becoming overwhelmed by supermarket shopping, whether you're spiralizing or not. Many of the following ingredients appear repeatedly in this cookbook because they offer easy, inexpensive ways to add a lot of flavour to a meal without extra calories, carbohydrates, or fat. With these items on hand, you'll always be able to create a nutritious meal.

EXTRA-VIRGIN OLIVE OIL: A heart-healthy fat, olive oil is great in everything from salad dressing to stir-fries. Most of my recipes begin with a tablespoon of olive oil, which helps meet your daily recommended serving of fat. Do keep in mind, however, that olive oil is high in calories and should be used in moderation if you are on a weight-loss journey.

EXTRA-VIRGIN COCONUT OIL: Coconuts are super-rich in nutrients. As an oil, they add a light coconut taste and associated nutrients to your meals, which is great in Asian sauces. This oil is high in calories and should be used in moderation if you are concerned about weight loss.

ASSORTED TINNED BEANS: I always keep my pantry stocked with cannellini beans, chickpeas, black beans, and kidney beans. They're a quick and easy protein source to add to any dish.

REDUCED-SALT CHICKEN, BEEF, AND VEGETABLE STOCK: Stock is a healthy way to add flavour to any vegetable noodle dish.

SESAME OIL: Toasted sesame oil is ideal for flavouring Asian dressings, stir-fries, and soups.

NUTS AND SEEDS: These both have the benefit of healthy fats and proteins. Add them to pastas, salads, and rices. I love sprinkling crushed pistachios over courgette pasta or adding pumpkin seeds to a pasta with black beans and avocado for a Mexican touch. Almonds, walnuts, cashews, peanuts, macadamia nuts, and Brazil nuts are all great choices!

CHUNK LIGHT TUNA (IN WATER): This type of tuna has the least amount of mercury. Packed in water, it also won't add unnecessary calories and fat from oil. Plus, it's a lean protein source that is ready to eat without cooking!

REDUCED-SALT SOY SAUCE: Soy sauce pairs well with sesame oil to make a quick Asian-inspired dish with lots of flavour for just a little prep time. Soy sauce is very high in salt, though, so be sure to get the reduced-salt kind.

RED WINE VINEGAR: Red wine vinegar is the ultimate ingredient for creating light salad dressings, thanks to its tangy, fresh taste and low calorie value.

BALSAMIC VINEGAR: Blame the Italian in me, but I think balsamic vinegar is the best! It makes an easy, tasty marinade that's low in calories and can be whisked into dressings to lend a tart kick.

APPLE CIDER VINEGAR: Made from apples instead of grapes, cider vinegar can be used in place of red wine vinegar or balsamic vinegar in dressings and marinades. It has incredible detoxifying and pH-balancing capabilities. Its sweeter taste is nice in raw salads, such as the Beetroot Superfood Bowl (page 140).

SPICES: I always cook with dried spices because they add flavour *and* nutrients. My favourites are chilli powder, oregano, smoked paprika, ground cumin, garlic powder, and crushed dried chillies.

SEA SALT AND PEPPERCORNS: These standard pantry items have a greater punch when freshly ground. If you want to make one great change to your kitchen pantry (and if you're not doing this already), it would be to throw away your salt and pepper shakers and replace them with grinders. Sea salt and peppercorns are less processed than the standard ones and are more flavourful. You'll wonder how you cooked without them!

JARS OF PASTA SAUCES: My grandparents might be horrified, but I always have jars of my favourite tomato-basil pasta sauce in my pantry for last-minute meals. Just be sure the ingredient list has whole tomatoes (and no sugar, no dairy, and preferably no added salt).

TINNED CHOPPED TOMATOES: When it's not summertime, tasty fresh tomatoes are hard to come by, so tinned chopped tomatoes tend to be preferable. Look for a no-salt-added variety.

OLIVE OIL COOKING SPRAY: Cooking spray is essential for coating baking sheets and it also works well for lightly sautéing vegetable noodles.

How to Use This Book

As you've realized, vegetable pasta is not only nutritious and filling but it's also easy to make. Spiralizing is for all ages, diet lifestyles, and cooking-skill levels. Even a university student in a hall of residence can make a big bowl of pasta using a spiralizer and the microwave!

I – a woman with an appetite for good food and a mind for healthy living – wrote all the recipes in this cookery book. They are easy to make and include ingredients that you can find in your local supermarket. Nothing is intended to be daunting or complicated. The inspiration for most of my recipes came from classic Italian pasta dishes that my grandparents cooked or food I tasted when dining out.

In an effort to present dishes that are truly healthy, you will not find the following ingredients in any of my recipes:

Butter	Mayonnaise
Dairy milk	Cream cheese
Cream	White breads
Sugar	

Can you make your fettuccini with whipping cream and your tomato cream sauce with butter? Of course, and it will be delicious. This cookbook is not just an alternative to wheat pasta; it is also a clean-eating cookbook with healthy sauces, lean meats, and moderate amounts of fats and carbohydrates. With this cookbook, you will be Inspiralizing whole meals, not just 'cooking' them! Experiment with these recipes; if you prefer the indulgent stuff, go ahead. Remember that part of healthy eating is moderation.

While I refrain from using most dairy products in my recipes, I do include some. Healthy living is all about what works for your own personal style. Cheese is an integral part of my family's culture and it's my biggest passion in cooking. I had to draw the line somewhere along my healthy journey, and that meant using cheese but only in moderation.

Recipe Features

Each recipe includes symbol indicators to give you a quick overview of its difficulty rating and nutritional information. First, the number of spirals is a measure of how difficult the recipe is to make:

≈ **ONE SPIRAL:** Very easy, not much cooking required, basic spiralizing

≈≈ **TWO SPIRALS:** Medium difficulty, more cooking required

≈≈≈ **THREE SPIRALS:** Most difficult, many steps required, more handling of the spiralized vegetables

However, don't let a three-spiral recipe intimidate you; it mostly just means that the recipe will take you a bit more time on account of the extra steps involved.

The spiralized ingredient in each recipe list follows this format:

1 medium courgette, spiralized with BLADE A

The vegetable should be spiralized *prior* to beginning the recipe, along with doing any other ingredient preparations, such as chopping and dicing. The ingredients are listed in the order in which they are used in the recipe. Whichever blade is specified is the one you should use to spiralize the vegetable. (See page 23 for a reminder of which blade does what.)

You'll also see some recipes classified as gluten-free, paleo, vegan, or vegetarian.

Ⓥ **VEGAN:** Does not contain any animal products

ⓋⓉ **VEGETARIAN:** Meat, poultry, and fowl-free, but may contain dairy and/or eggs

ⒼⒻ **GLUTEN-FREE:** Does not contain any gluten

Ⓟ **PALEO:** Excludes dairy, grain products, and any processed food

And finally, all recipes include the following nutritional information: calories, fat, carbohydrates, salt, protein, and sugar for the stated portion size.

Now, are you excited to eat? Grab your spiralizer and join me as we revolutionize the way we regard vegetables. We're going to have fun, whittle down our waistlines, and tantalize and surprise our taste buds. This book was written with passion, love, and commitment to living a lifestyle that satisfies the tummy and supports a healthy heart and mind. What would I call that lifestyle? *Inspiralized.*

BREAKFASTS

Chorizo and Avocado Courgette Frittata
with Manchego-Pea Shoot Salad

Pesto Sun-Dried Tomato Egg Muffins

Blueberry Sweet Potato Waffles

Ham and Swede Breakfast in a Frying Pan

Cinnamon-Walnut Protein Muffins

Huevos Rancheros

'Bagel' Breakfast Buns

Savoy Cabbage Breakfast Burrito

Kohlrabi and Sausage Breakfast Sauté
with Spicy Salsa Verde

Chorizo and Avocado Courgette Frittata with Manchego-Pea Shoot Salad

MAKES
4 servings

GF

TIME TO PREPARE
20 minutes

TIME TO COOK
25 minutes

NUTRITIONAL INFORMATION
SERVING SIZE: ¼ **frittata +**
¼ **recipe salad**
Calories: 451
Fat: 32g
Carbohydrates: 24g
Salt: 1g
Protein: 48g
Sugar: 11g

ALSO WORKS WITH
Kohlrabi • Potatoes •
Parsnips • Beetroot

If you've never put leftover pasta into a frittata, now's your time to try it – but with courgette noodles. These noodles add texture, heartiness, and nutrients. The mild cheese and dainty yet tangy pea shoots are perfect accompaniments for this spicy and rich frittata. I like to make the frittata as 'breakfast for dinner', but it will certainly wow any guests for brunch, with the spirals of courgette peeking through the baked eggs.

For the frittata

Cooking spray

2 spicy chorizo sausages, casings removed, meat crumbled

1 avocado, cubed

1 large garlic clove, very finely chopped

2 medium courgettes, spiralized with BLADE C

3 medium eggs plus 9 egg whites, lightly beaten

Salt and pepper

For the salad

2 tablespoons lemon juice

3 tablespoons olive oil

2 tablespoons sherry vinegar

2 teaspoons honey

Salt and pepper

300g diced pea shoots

30g diced manchego cheese

If you can't find pea shoots for the salad, use watercress instead.

1 Make the frittata. Preheat the oven to 190°C/375°F. Coat a large ovenproof frying pan with cooking spray and place over a medium heat. When water flicked onto the pan sizzles, add the chorizo, avocado, and garlic and cook for 5 minutes or until the chorizo crumbles begin to brown. Add the courgette noodles and toss to combine. Spread the ingredients in an even layer.

2 Pour the eggs over the noodles and season to taste with salt and pepper. Cook for 2 minutes or until the eggs are set on the bottom, then transfer the frying pan to the oven and bake for about 15 minutes or until the eggs have completely set and begin to brown on the edges.

3 Make the salad. Whisk together the lemon juice, olive oil, sherry, honey, and salt and pepper in a small bowl. Toss with the pea shoots and manchego.

4 Slice the frittata into 4 or 8 pieces. Serve with the pea shoot salad.

Pesto Sun-Dried Tomato Egg Muffins

MAKES
6 muffins

TIME TO PREPARE
15 minutes

TIME TO COOK
25 minutes

NUTRITIONAL INFORMATION
SERVING SIZE: 1 muffin + 1 heaped tablespoon pesto
Calories: 303
Fat: 24g
Carbohydrates: 13g
Salt: 0.2g
Protein: 11g
Sugar: 1g

ALSO WORKS WELL WITH
Courgettes

Usually when I make the trip to my parents' home in New Jersey for a birthday or similar celebration, my mother serves brunch. From the crockery to the table spread, she always makes these occasions special. She once prepared the most adorable egg muffins, which inspired this recipe. They take the presentation up a notch – the potato noodles are visible from the outside, which is a conversation starter. They are also a complete meal, with your protein, starch, and vegetables all in one!

1 Preheat the oven to 190°C/375°F.

2 Make the pesto. Combine the ingredients in a food processor and purée to a thick paste, periodically scraping down the sides. Transfer to a container and keep covered so the pesto does not brown.

3 Make the muffins. Heat the olive oil in a large non-stick frying pan over a medium heat. When the oil is shimmering, add the potato noodles and season with the garlic powder, salt, and pepper. Cover and cook for 6–8 minutes, tossing occasionally, until the noodles wilt and begin to brown. When the noodles are cooked through, remove from the frying pan and set aside. Using the same frying pan, again over a medium heat, add the spinach and cook until wilted, a minute or two.

For the pesto
100g fresh basil leaves

30g pine nuts

60ml olive oil

Salt and pepper

1 large garlic clove, finely chopped

For the muffins
1 tablespoon olive oil

1 large Maris Piper potato, peeled, spiralized with BLADE C

1 teaspoon garlic powder

Salt and pepper

175g fresh baby spinach

Olive oil or cooking spray

7 medium eggs, lightly beaten

20g sun-dried tomatoes, finely chopped

4 Coat a 6-hole non-stick muffin tin with olive oil or cooking spray. To each hole, add 1.5cm of beaten egg. Then add about 2.5cm of the potato noodles. Top each with a few leaves of wilted spinach and 1 tablespoon of the sun-dried tomato. Slowly pour the remaining egg on top until the cups are full. Generously sprinkle the tops with more pepper.

5 Bake for 15 minutes or until the eggs are set. Remove from the oven, allow to cool in the muffin tin for 1 minute, then carefully remove the muffins and serve, each drizzled with a bit of pesto.

For a quicker-to-make and lighter muffin, use courgette noodles instead of potato. The courgette doesn't need to be seasoned or cooked beforehand; it simply adds a nice crunch to the muffin.

Blueberry Sweet Potato Waffles

MAKES
2 waffles

GF

TIME TO PREPARE
15 minutes

VT

TIME TO COOK
10 minutes

P

NUTRITIONAL INFORMATION
SERVING SIZE: **1 waffle +
½ tablespoon pure
maple syrup**
Calories: 150
Fat: 3g
Carbohydrates: 28g
Salt: 0.2g
Protein: 4g
Sugar: 13g

These waffles are as clean eating as it gets. When you take your first bite, you will taste the plump blueberries, spicy cinnamon, and soft sweet potato. Instead of using flour, sugar, and butter – or worse, something frozen in a box – try this recipe. While they don't have the fluffiness of traditional waffles, they do offer an interesting texture, and the natural sugar in the sweet potatoes gives them a special sweetness. With warmed blueberries and maple syrup to accompany, these waffles are sure to become a brunch favourite.

1 Preheat a waffle iron. Place the sweet potato noodles in a bowl and toss with the cinnamon. Place a large frying pan over a medium heat and coat with cooking spray. When water flicked onto the frying pan sizzles, add the seasoned sweet potato noodles and cover. Cook for 5–7 minutes or until the noodles have completely softened.

2 Transfer the noodles to a large bowl and add the egg, vanilla extract, and blueberries. Toss gently to combine until the noodles are coated, taking care not to break them.

3 Coat the waffle iron with cooking spray and carefully pour in half of the noodle mixture, taking care to fill all the cavities with noodles. Cook the waffle following the manufacturer's instructions. When the waffle is done, transfer to a plate and keep warm while you make the second waffle. Drizzle a bit of maple syrup over each and serve.

1 medium sweet potato, peeled,
    spiralized with **BLADE C**

1 teaspoon ground cinnamon

Cooking spray

1 medium egg, lightly beaten

½ teaspoon vanilla extract

60g fresh blueberries

1 tablespoon maple syrup or to taste

Add dairy-free chocolate chips for extra sweetness.

Ham and Swede Breakfast in a Frying Pan

MAKES
4–6 servings

TIME TO PREPARE
10 minutes

TIME TO COOK
35 minutes

NUTRITIONAL INFORMATION
SERVING SIZE: 1/4 **recipe**
Calories: 171
Fat: 8g
Carbohydrates: 10g
Salt: 1.6g
Protein: 14g
Sugar: 7g

ALSO WORKS WELL WITH
Sweet Potatoes

You might not typically eat rice for breakfast, but when it's this spiralized rice, you'll welcome the change in routine. Starting off your morning with a hefty serving of vegetables ensures a productive and focused day. The eggs bake nestled in the swede-rice mixture and, when broken to serve, coat the rice and ham with a warm, yolky sauce. Every bite is slightly sweet and comforting.

1 Preheat the oven to 200°C/400°F. Heat the olive oil in a large non-stick ovenproof frying pan over a medium heat. Add the garlic, onion, and crushed dried chillies. Cook for 2 minutes or until the onion is translucent. Add the swede rice, ham, kale, paprika, cumin, and tomatoes. Stir to combine well and season with
salt and pepper. Add the stock and cook for 2–3 minutes more, or until reduced somewhat, stirring occasionally.

2 Create four evenly spaced cavities in the mixture and crack an egg into each. Transfer to the oven and bake for about 10 minutes or until the eggs are set.

3 Serve hot, family-style, sprinkled with parsley.

1 tablespoon olive oil

2 large garlic cloves, finely chopped

115g white onion, chopped

Pinch of crushed dried chillies

1 small swede, peeled, spiralized with
   BLADE C, then riced (see page 25)

120g cooked ham, cut into cubes

50g fresh kale, chopped

1 teaspoon smoked paprika

1 teaspoon ground cumin

165g ripe tomatoes, chopped, with juices

Salt and pepper

120ml reduced-salt chicken stock

4 medium eggs

1 tablespoon chopped fresh parsley

Cinnamon-Walnut Protein Muffins

MAKES
4 large muffins

GF

TIME TO PREPARE
10 minutes

VT

TIME TO COOK
25 minutes

P

NUTRITIONAL INFORMATION
SERVING SIZE: **1 muffin**
Calories: 130
Fat: 6g
Carbohydrates: 17g
Salt: 0.3g
Protein: 4g
Sugar: 9g

I hadn't used protein powder until I started drinking smoothies for breakfast. One day I added some and I just never stopped – it kept me feeling full for much longer. Now, I even add protein powder to baked goods. Keep yourself nourished and satisfied all morning with these flavourful and sweet muffins.

1 Preheat the oven to 190°C/375°F. Combine the sweet potato rice, cinnamon, protein powder, and bicarbonate of soda in a medium bowl. Add the egg, honey, and vanilla extract, and mix thoroughly. Stir in the raisins and walnuts and mix again.

2 Coat a large 6-hole muffin tin lightly with cooking spray. Spoon the batter evenly into 4 holes and bake for 23–25 minutes or until a cocktail stick inserted into the centre comes out clean. Remove from the oven and let the tin sit for a minute or two, then invert to remove the muffins. Allow to cool for 5 minutes before eating.

1 medium sweet potato, peeled, spiralized with BLADE C, then riced (see page 25)

¼ teaspoon ground cinnamon

1 tablespoon protein powder

¼ teaspoon bicarbonate of soda

1 medium egg

1 tablespoon honey

¼ teaspoon vanilla extract

2 tablespoons raisins

25g chopped walnuts

Cooking spray

If you use a vanilla-flavoured protein powder, skip the vanilla extract here. I prefer plant-based protein powders, such as those derived from peas or brown rice.

Huevos Rancheros

MAKES
2 servings

GF

TIME TO PREPARE
20 minutes

VT

TIME TO COOK
25 minutes

NUTRITIONAL INFORMATION
**SERVING SIZE: 1 plantain
tortilla with sauce +
1 egg and toppings**
Calories: 623
Fat: 32g
Carbohydrates: 69g
Salt: 0.9g
Protein: 22g
Sugar: 23g

Huevos rancheros are Lu's go-to meal when we're out for brunch. The plantain rice tortilla serves as the fried tortilla, and it's both more flavourful and lower in saturated fat than the usual. As my official taste tester and huevos rancheros expert, Lu approves of this recipe and I know you will, too.

For the tortillas and roasted sweetcorn

Cooking spray

1 medium-ripe plantain, peeled, spiralized with **BLADE C**, then riced (see page 25)

1 medium egg

1 tablespoon coconut flakes

Salt and pepper

1 ear of sweetcorn, husked and silks removed

Chilli powder

For the ranchero sauce

1 tablespoon olive oil

1 teaspoon finely chopped garlic

60g white onion, chopped

1 teaspoon tomato purée

80g tinned chopped tomatoes, with juice

80g tinned black beans, drained and rinsed

1 avocado, cubed

1 teaspoon chilli powder

1 tablespoon finely chopped deseeded jalapeño pepper

1 tablespoon chopped fresh coriander

1 teaspoon ground cumin

1 teaspoon dried Mexican seasoning or oregano

Salt and pepper

To finish the dish

30g Monterey Jack or Cheddar cheese, grated

Cooking spray

2 medium eggs

These huevos rancheros still taste incredible without the cheese, so if you're watching your waistline or are dairy-free, just skip the cheese.

(recipe continues)

1 Preheat the oven to 200°C/400°F.

2 Make the tortillas. Line one baking sheet with parchment paper and lightly coat a second sheet with cooking spray.

3 Place the plantain rice in a bowl and add the egg and coconut flakes. Stir to combine thoroughly and season with salt and pepper. Scoop out half of the mixture and place it on one side of the lined baking sheet. Using your hands, flatten the mixture and round the edges to make it like a tortilla. Repeat with the remaining mixture on the opposite end of the lined baking sheet.

4 Place the sweetcorn on the coated baking sheet and generously season with salt, pepper, and chilli powder. Transfer both baking sheets to the oven. Bake the plantain tortillas for 15–17 minutes or until they are firm and golden brown on top. Remove the sweetcorn when it's easily pierced with a fork,12–15 minutes.

5 Prepare the ranchero sauce. Heat the olive oil in a medium saucepan over a medium-low heat. When the oil is shimmering, add the garlic. Cook for 30 seconds or until fragrant, then add the onion, tomato purée, and tomatoes. Cook for 2–3 minutes, until the tomato sauce begins to reduce. Add half the beans, the avocado, chilli powder, jalapeño, coriander, cumin, and Mexican seasoning. Season with salt and pepper. Reduce the heat and simmer for about 5 minutes or until sauce thickens to a creamy consistency.

6 While the sauce cooks, mash the remaining beans with a fork or potato masher.

7 Finish the dish. Transfer the plantain tortillas to a large ovenproof frying pan. (If they both don't fit, use two small frying pans.) Mix the mashed beans with the ranchero sauce and divide the mixture evenly between the tortillas, then top with the cheese and bake for 5 minutes or until the cheese melts.

8 Place a large non-stick frying pan over a medium heat and coat with cooking spray. When a bit of water flicked onto the frying pan sizzles, crack in the 2 eggs and fry until the whites are set, about 3 minutes.

9 Transfer the tortillas to serving plates. Slice the corn kernels off the cob and divide most of the kernels evenly over the tortillas. Top each tortilla with a fried egg, then garnish with the remaining corn kernels and serve.

'Bagel' Breakfast Buns

MAKES
4 buns

GF

TIME TO PREPARE
15 minutes

TIME TO COOK
25 minutes

NUTRITIONAL INFORMATION
SERVING SIZE: 1 bun
Calories: 170
Fat: 9g
Carbohydrates: 19g
Salt: 0.6g
Protein: 5g
Sugar: 2g

ALSO WORKS WELL WITH
Sweet Potatoes

If you ask most kids who grew up in New Jersey what their favourite breakfast is, they'll most likely come back with "ham, egg, and cheese on a bagel." The mere scent of this doughy breakfast favourite makes me recall those wonderful mornings when my mother would bring home a fresh batch from the local shop. Of course, I had to Inspiralize this iconic American breakfast choice.

1 Make the bagel mix. Combine the ingredients in a small bowl and set aside.

2 Make the buns. Heat a large non-stick frying pan over a medium heat and coat with cooking spray. When water flicked onto the frying pan sizzles, add the potato noodles and season with salt and pepper. Cover and cook, tossing occasionally, for 5–7 minutes or until the potatoes are golden brown. Transfer to a large bowl and allow to cool for 2 minutes.

3 Stir in the eggs and bagel mix. Toss until the potato noodles are evenly coated. Fill four 10 x 4.5cm ramekins halfway with the potato noodles. Cover each with a piece of aluminum foil or greaseproof paper, pressing it firmly down onto the potato noodles to compress them. Refrigerate for at least 15 minutes to set.

For the bagel mix
1 teaspoon poppy seeds

1 teaspoon sesame seeds

1¼ teaspoons garlic powder

1 teaspoon onion powder

½ teaspoon coarse sea salt

¼ teaspoon freshly cracked black peppercorns

For the buns
Cooking spray

1 large Maris Piper potato, peeled, spiralized with BLADE C

Salt and pepper

1 medium egg and 1 egg white, lightly beaten

2 tablespoons olive oil

(recipe continues)

4 Heat 1 tablespoon of the olive oil in a large non-stick frying pan over a medium heat. When the oil is shimmering, add the buns two at a time, flipping each out of its ramekin into the frying pan and patting the bottom until the bun falls out. Cook for 3 minutes or until set, being sure to push in any stray noodles. Carefully flip and cook another 2 to 3 minutes or until the buns are completely set and browned on both sides. Repeat with the other ramekins, adding the remaining tablespoon of oil as needed.

5 Serve the bagel buns with spreads and toppings of your choice.

If you don't have the right size ramekins, you can still make this and other bun recipes. Just heat $1/2$ tablespoon olive oil in a frying pan, and instead of packing the noodles into a ramekin and refrigerating, put one-quarter of the mixture in the middle of the frying pan. Immediately form it into a patty and flatten with a spatula, taking care to keep the noodles tightly packed. Flip the patty after about 2 minutes, or after the bottom sets, and cook for another 2 minutes, flattening again with the back of a spatula.

Savoy Cabbage Breakfast Burrito

MAKES
2 burritos

TIME TO PREPARE
10 minutes

TIME TO COOK
15 minutes

NUTRITIONAL INFORMATION
SERVING SIZE: 1 burrito
Calories: 420
Fat: 27g
Carbohydrates: 24g
Salt: 1.5g
Protein: 22g
Sugar: 5g

ALSO WORKS WELL WITH
Swede • Beetroot •
Carrots • Parsnips

Nothing says breakfast like bacon, eggs, and potatoes. But how do you put a new twist on such basic ingredients? You spiralize them into a burrito! Burritos are great because they can be prepped in advance and are easily transported – you can wrap this bad boy in aluminium foil and eat it on the road, at work, at a picnic, or wherever. The savoy cabbage works wonders here, keeping all the ingredients intact without breaking apart. Plus, you're getting your greens first thing in the morning. Top the burrito with Sriracha or ketchup for even more flavour.

1 In a small bowl, mash the avocado and season with salt and pepper. Spread half the avocado mixture in the centre of each cabbage leaf.

2 Place a large non-stick frying pan over a medium heat. When a little water flicked onto the frying pan sizzles, add the bacon. Cook until crisped to your liking, then set aside on a kitchen paper-lined plate to drain.

3 Discard half the fat from the pan and add the sweet potato noodles. Cover and cook over a medium heat, tossing occasionally, for 5–8 minutes or until wilted. Divide the noodles evenly between the cabbage leaves, layering them over the avocado.

4 In the same frying pan, still over a medium heat, crack the eggs and scramble, cooking until set. Spread the eggs over the sweet potato noodles. Top each wrap with two pieces of bacon. Roll up like a burrito and serve.

1 avocado, cubed

Salt and pepper

2 leaves of savoy cabbage

4 rashers streaky bacon

1 sweet potato, peeled, spiralized
with **BLADE C**

4 medium eggs, lightly beaten

If you'd like to turn this wrap into a more traditional rice-based burrito, place the sweet potato noodles into a food processor and pulse until rice-like. Then, toss them in a frying pan with some coconut or extra-virgin olive oil and salt and pepper for 5–7 minutes or until cooked through. Add them to the mix and roll up like a burrito!

Kohlrabi and Sausage Breakfast Sauté with Spicy Salsa Verde

MAKES
2 servings

GF

P

TIME TO PREPARE
15 minutes

TIME TO COOK
10 minutes

NUTRITIONAL INFORMATION
SERVING SIZE: ½ of pasta
recipe + 2 chicken
sausages
Calories: 170
Fat: 18g
Carbohydrates: 19g
Salt: 0.6g
Protein: 5g
Sugar: 2g

ALSO WORKS WELL WITH
Courgettes

During the week, I'm pretty regular about my breakfast: a green protein smoothie or Greek yogurt with granola and blueberries. But on the weekends it's a totally different ball game. Breakfast becomes brunch, and I can pack in the vegetables and all of my favourite breakfast foods in one shot. This kohlrabi breakfast sauté will change the way you view breakfast. Yes, you can eat noodles for breakfast, and no, I'm not talking about leftover lo mein! Climb out of your own breakfast rut and whip up this dish – your body will be fuelled for the day with tons of potassium and dietary fibre. The mild, crunchy kohlrabi perfectly absorbs the flavours of the egg, sausage, and salsa.

For the salsa verde
  2 medium tomatillos, husks removed, rinsed, or underripe tomatoes
  2 tablespoons fresh lime juice
  Salt
  2 teaspoons diced jalapeño pepper
  2 tablespoons chopped white onion
  15g fresh coriander

To save time, use your favourite tinned salsa; just warm it in a small saucepan first.

For the sauté
  Cooking spray
  2 medium eggs, lightly beaten
  1 tablespoon olive oil
  4 small apple-flavoured chicken sausages, sliced into 6mm-thick rounds
  40g white onion, chopped
  1 small garlic clove, finely chopped
  1 large kohlrabi (about 150g), peeled, spiralized with BLADE C
  Salt and pepper
  120g endive (or fresh spinach or rocket)

1 Make the salsa verde. Place the tomatillos in a small saucepan and just cover with water. Bring to the boil over a high heat, then reduce to low and simmer for about 10 minutes or until the tomatillos soften and turn light green. Drain in a colander, then place in a food processor along with the lime juice, salt, jalapeño, onion, and coriander. Blend until the mixture reaches your desired consistency and season with salt to taste.

2 Make the sauté. Place a large non-stick frying pan over a medium heat and coat with cooking spray. When a bit of water flicked onto the frying pan sizzles, add the eggs and scramble until set. Transfer to a bowl.

3 Add the olive oil to the frying pan, still over a medium heat. When the oil is shimmering, add the chicken sausage, onion, and garlic. Cook for 2–3 minutes or until the onion is translucent.

4 Add the kohlrabi noodles, season with salt and pepper, and cook for 3–5 minutes, tossing frequently, until the noodles soften to *al dente*. Halfway through the cooking, add the greens and toss to combine.

5 Return the scrambled eggs to the frying pan to warm them for about a minute. Divide the mixture evenly between two bowls and drizzle each with the spicy salsa.

SNACKS & SIDES

Spicy Sweet Potato Strings

Cucumber, Avocado, and Strawberry Salsa

Spicy Butternut Squash Nachos

Pears with Farro, Cherries, Walnuts, and Goat's Cheese

Lemon Garlic Broccoli with Bacon

Baked Onion Bhaji with Mint-Cucumber Raita

Balsamic Glazed Peaches with Prosciutto and Roquefort

Apple and Kohlrabi Slaw with Lemon-Mint
Chia Seed Dressing

Beetroot, Goat's Cheese, and Pomegranate Chicory Cups

Mango-Avocado Cucumber Spring Rolls with
Sriracha-Lime Dipping Sauce

Spicy Sweet Potato Strings

MAKES
5 servings

TIME TO PREPARE
10 minutes

TIME TO COOK
25 minutes

NUTRITIONAL INFORMATION
SERVING SIZE: $^1/_5$ **recipe**
Calories: 97
Fat: 5g
Carbohydrates: 11g
Salt: 0.1g
Protein: 1g
Sugar: 3g

ALSO WORKS WELL WITH
Potatoes • Swedes •
Parsnips • Kohlrabi •
Celeriac

The spiralizer can easily be used to make curly, thick-cut, or shoestring chips. You can fry them or bake them in the oven to re-create your favourite fast food. But there's nothing special about that, is there? These sweet potato strings are different, though. I call them 'strings' because they're meant to be floppier and not quite as crisp as typical chips. These strings are perfect for topping burgers or salads, or for eating as a side dish!

1 Preheat the oven to 200°C/400°F. Spread the sweet potato noodles on two large baking sheets, drizzle with olive oil, and toss to coat well. Season generously with salt, the onion powder, cayenne pepper, and chilli powder and toss again. Spread in an even layer.

2 Bake for 15 minutes, then flip and bake another 10–15 minutes or until the strings reach your preferred crispness.

1 large sweet potato, peeled, spiralized with **BLADE C**

2 tablespoons olive oil

Salt

1 tablespoon onion powder

2 teaspoons cayenne pepper

2 teaspoons chilli powder

Prior to baking the sweet potato noodles, be sure to cut them into smaller pieces, no longer than 7.5cm. To make these a bit crisper, blanch them for a minute in boiling water, then spread them in an even layer and bake at 230°C/450°F.

Cucumber, Avocado, and Strawberry Salsa

MAKES
4–6 servings

 GF

TIME TO PREPARE
15 minutes

 V

P

NUTRITIONAL INFORMATION
SERVING SIZE: $1/4$ **recipe**
Calories: 90
Fat: 5g
Carbohydrates: 14g
Salt: 0g
Protein: 2g
Sugar: 7g

Who says salsa has to have perfectly cubed ingredients? Not those of us who are Inspiralized! It's time to transform your salsas by using cucumber half-moons. Whenever I'm invited to a barbecue or sporting event, where I know healthy foods will be scarce, I bring this filling snack. Not only is it fun to eat, but it's also a conversation starter.

1 Slice the cucumber in half lengthways. Spiralize using blade C. Pat the cucumber noodles dry to absorb moisture.

2 In a large bowl, combine the cucumber noodles, strawberries, avocado, coriander, jalapeño, and red onion. In a small bowl, whisk together the honey and lime juice and season with salt and pepper. Pour the dressing over the salsa and toss with the cucumber mixture to combine. Serve with crisps or vegetable crudités.

1 large seedless cucumber

200g hulled and chopped fresh strawberries

1 very ripe avocado, diced

1 tablespoon chopped fresh coriander

1 small jalapeño pepper, deseeded and finely chopped

30g red onion, finely chopped

1 teaspoon honey

Juice of 1 lime

Salt and pepper

If you're preparing this salsa in advance, add the cucumber noodles at the last minute to avoid a build-up of moisture.

Spicy Butternut Squash Nachos

MAKES
4–6 servings

GF

TIME TO PREPARE
25 minutes

VT

TIME TO COOK
35 minutes

NUTRITIONAL INFORMATION
SERVING SIZE: 1/4 **recipe**
Calories: 246
Fat: 9g
Carbohydrates: 36g
Salt: 0.5g
Protein: 8g
Sugar: 7g

ALSO WORKS WELL WITH
Sweet Potatoes •
Beetroot

Whenever my parents would visit me at university, my father would insist that we eat at The Village Tavern, a local restaurant. Why? He was crazy for their nachos. Those nachos were beyond fully loaded and worth every bite. By the time we were done with dinner, though, we each were yearning to go lie belly-up on a sofa. This slimmed-down version induces that same 'Yes, nachos!' feeling without the subsequent bloat. The butternut squash crisps replace the corn tortilla crisps, and they nourish you while providing that salty crunch. Even my father approves!

For the crisps
1 small-to-medium butternut squash, peeled

Olive oil, for brushing

Salt and pepper

1 teaspoon chilli powder

For the topping
1 ear of sweetcorn, husked and silks removed

Olive oil, for brushing

Salt and pepper

1/2 teaspoon chilli powder

For the avocado salsa
135g cubed avocado

2 ripe tomatoes, deseeded and chopped

1 jalapeño pepper, deseeded and finely chopped

1 small white onion, diced

2 tablespoons chopped fresh coriander

1 tablespoon lime juice

Salt and pepper

For the bean topping
2 teaspoons olive oil

1 small garlic clove, finely chopped

225g tinned kidney beans, drained and rinsed

60g pitted black olives, quartered

1/2 teaspoon ground cumin

1/4 teaspoon dried oregano

4 tablespoons grated Monterey Jack cheese

4 tablespoons grated mature Cheddar cheese

Using a small-to-medium butternut squash will yield the perfect crisp size. A larger butternut squash will give you wider, larger slices, which won't work as well in this dish.

1 Make the crisps. Preheat the oven to 190°C/375°F. Line two baking sheets with parchment paper and set aside. Bring a medium pot of salted water to the boil.

2 Cut the squash lengthways in half and spiralize using blade A. Drop the slices into the boiling water and cook for exactly 2 minutes. Drain and pat dry to remove excess moisture. Arrange the slices in an even layer on one of the baking sheets and brush both sides with olive oil. Season generously with salt, pepper, and the chilli powder and toss to combine. Bake for 25–30 minutes or until crisp, turning halfway through and taking care not to burn the crisps.

3 Prepare the sweetcorn. Brush with a little olive oil and sprinkle with salt and pepper and the chilli powder. Bake the sweetcorn for 12 minutes or until it turns deep yellow. Remove the sweetcorn from the oven and allow it to cool for a few minutes before slicing the kernels off the cob.

4 Make the salsa. Combine the ingredients in a medium bowl.

5 Prepare the bean topping. Heat the olive oil in a large non-stick frying pan over a medium heat. When the oil is shimmering, add the garlic and cook for 30 seconds or until fragrant. Add the beans, olives, cumin, and oregano. Cook for 2–3 minutes, stirring frequently, or until the beans break down slightly and the vegetables have warmed through. Transfer the bean mixture to a medium bowl and toss in the corn kernels.

6 When the crisps are firm, remove the baking sheet from the oven, but leave the oven on. Place half the crisps in the bottom of a large baking dish. Layer over half of the bean topping, then the remaining crisps. Finish with the remaining bean topping and sprinkle evenly with the cheeses. Put the baking dish in the oven and bake for 10–15 minutes or until the cheese melts. Remove from the oven, top with the avocado salsa, and serve immediately.

Pears with Farro, Cherries, Walnuts, and Goat's Cheese

MAKES
3–4 servings

VT

TIME TO PREPARE
10 minutes

TIME TO COOK
20 minutes

NUTRITIONAL INFORMATION
SERVING SIZE: ¼ **recipe**
Calories: 348
Fat: 18g
Carbohydrates: 42g
Salt: 0.3g
Protein: 8g
Sugar: 17g

Despite the fact that this cookbook is devoted to vegetable substitutes for rice and noodles, that doesn't mean I never eat grains. On the contrary! Farro is one of my favourites, with its pleasant chewiness and lovely nutty flavour. The creaminess of the goat's cheese and the sweetness of the cherries and pear noodles complement its *al dente* texture. I always keep a bag of farro to hand, and I love mixing it into salads and vegetable dishes. My grandfather introduced me to farro, claiming that it fed the Roman legions. If it's okay for the Romans, it's okay for me!

1 Bring the water to the boil in a large saucepan over a high heat. Add the farro and a pinch of salt. Cook for 15 minutes or until the farro is *al dente*. Drain well.

2 Place the walnuts in a medium non-stick frying pan over a medium heat and toast for 2–3 minutes or until fragrant and lightly browned.

3 Make the dressing. Pulse all the ingredients in a food processor until emulsified and evenly incorporated.

4 Combine the farro, pear noodles, walnuts, and cherries in a large bowl. Pour the dressing on top and toss to combine. Transfer to a serving bowl and top with the goat's cheese.

If you're grain-free, substitute shredded chard or spinach for the farro.

950ml water

140g uncooked farro

Salt

60g walnuts, chopped

For the dressing

1 tablespoon honey

1 tablespoon balsamic vinegar

Salt and pepper

2 tablespoons olive oil

2 tablespoons lemon juice

1 tablespoon wholegrain or Dijon mustard

2 teaspoons finely chopped fresh parsley

2 medium firm, crunchy pears, spiralized with BLADE C

200g sweet fresh cherries, stoned and halved

60g goat's cheese, crumbled

Lemon Garlic Broccoli with Bacon

MAKES
4 servings

GF

TIME TO PREPARE
5 minutes

TIME TO COOK
15 minutes

NUTRITIONAL INFORMATION
SERVING SIZE: ¼ **recipe**
Calories: 305
Fat: 12g
Carbohydrates: 33g
Salt: 0.8g
Protein: 16g
Sugar: 8g

ALSO WORKS WELL WITH
Courgettes

My grandfather makes an unbelievably simple dish with garlic, olive oil, and broccoli. Basically, the broccoli floats in a pool of olive oil; when you pierce a floret with your fork, you have to let it drip-dry for a moment before eating it! As much as I love his version, it always leaves me with a slight tummy ache. This recipe brings in extra flavour from the bacon while minimizing the amount of olive oil. Also, it uses the entire broccoli, stem and all! It's a recipe that showcases the extreme versatility of the spiralizer and what it empowers you to make out of everyday vegetables.

1 Fill a large saucepan halfway with salted water and bring to the boil over a high heat. Add the broccoli florets and broccoli noodles. Cook for 2–3 minutes or until easily pierced with a fork. Drain and pat dry.

2 Place a large frying pan over a medium heat and coat with cooking spray. When water flicked onto the frying pan sizzles, add the bacon rashers in an even layer, working in batches if needed, and cook for 3 minutes per side or until browned and crisp to your liking. Set aside on a kitchen paper-lined plate to drain.

3 Wipe out the frying pan, return it to a medium heat, and add the olive oil. When the oil is shimmering, add the broccoli florets, broccoli noodles, and crushed dried chillies; season with salt and pepper. Cover and cook for 2 minutes, uncovering occasionally to toss. Add the garlic, lemon juice, and zest; cover and cook for another 5 minutes or until the broccoli is lightly browned.

4 Remove the pan from the heat and stir in the cheese. Toss to combine and serve warm.

3 large broccoli heads with stems (see Tip)

Cooking spray

6 rashers streaky bacon

2 tablespoons olive oil

¼ teaspoon crushed dried chillies

Salt and pepper

5 medium garlic cloves, thinly sliced

Juice of 1 lemon and zest of half a lemon

3 tablespoons grated Parmesan cheese

Slice off the broccoli florets, leaving as little stem as possible, and set aside. Then spiralize the stems using blade C.

Baked Onion Bhaji with Mint-Cucumber Raita

GF

VT

MAKES
4–6 bhajis

TIME TO PREPARE
15 minutes

TIME TO COOK
45 minutes

NUTRITIONAL INFORMATION
SERVING SIZE: 1 bhaji and 2 tablespoons of raita
Calories: 91
Fat: 3g
Carbohydrates: 9g
Salt: 0.1g
Protein: 5g
Sugar: 4g

ALSO WORKS WELL WITH
Potatoes

One of the easiest ways to revamp your beloved fried foods is to bake them. The onion *bhaji*, also sometimes called a *pakora*, depending on the region, is India's version of a British or American fritter. Typically crispy and sinfully delicious, this Inspiralized version is whipped up quickly using spiralized onions, and because it is baked, it has much less saturated fat. Instead of eliminating unwholesome foods from your diet, you can always find a way to make a cleaner version!

For the bhajis
Cooking spray

1 medium onion, peeled, spiralized with **BLADE A**

¼ teaspoon chilli powder

½ teaspoon ground turmeric

¼ teaspoon ground cumin

¼ teaspoon ground ginger

2 teaspoons finely chopped fresh coriander

50g chickpea flour or coconut flour

1 medium egg, lightly beaten

½ tablespoon olive oil

Salt and pepper

2–3 lemons, quartered for garnish

For the raita
¼ medium cucumber, chopped

115g natural 0% fat Greek yogurt

1 teaspoon chopped fresh mint leaves

1 teaspoon fresh lemon juice

Salt and pepper

1 Make the bhajis. Preheat the oven to 200°C/400°F. Line a baking sheet with parchment paper and coat with cooking spray.

2 Heat a large non-stick frying pan over a medium heat. When a little water flicked onto the frying pan sizzles, add the onion and cook for 3–4 minutes or until beginning to turn translucent. Transfer to a bowl to cool for 2–3 minutes.

3 In a medium bowl, combine the chilli powder, turmeric, cumin, ginger, coriander, and flour. Add the egg and the cooked onion and mix well. If the mixture appears too dry, gradually add warm water, 1 tablespoon at a time.

4 Working with one-quarter of the mixture at a time, transfer the mixture to the parchment paper, using the back of a spatula to flatten into discs. Brush the tops of the bhajis with olive oil and season with salt and pepper. Bake for 40 minutes or until golden brown, flipping over halfway through.

5 Prepare your raita. Press out the extra moisture in the cucumber with kitchen paper and finely chop. Add the cucumber to a medium bowl along with the rest of the ingredients and mix well. Season with salt and pepper to taste.

6 To serve, squeeze a lemon quarter over each bhaji and serve with raita alongside.

For an extra-crispy outside on your bhajis, use an ovenproof cast-iron frying pan coated with a tablespoon of olive oil, instead of a baking sheet. The olive oil will bubble up and 'fry' them in the oven.

Balsamic Glazed Peaches with Prosciutto and Roquefort

GF

VT

MAKES
16 hors d'oeuvres

TIME TO PREPARE
20 minutes

TIME TO COOK
15 minutes

NUTRITIONAL INFORMATION
SERVING SIZE: **1 peach slice with a drizzle of balsamic glaze and a crumbling of Roquefort**
Calories: 86
Fat: 4g
Carbohydrates: 6g
Salt: 0.3g
Protein: 5g
Sugar: 6g

My mother taught me to never arrive at someone's home empty-handed. The polite thing is to bring a bottle of wine or some flowers. But, why not *really* make an impression by walking through the door with these hors d'oeuvres? The prosciutto-wrapped seared peaches are sophisticated and best for summertime. The courgette ribbons are purely decorative, but they add colour and some fun. Whether you're serving these at your own soirée or bringing them to a friend, they'll be the talk of the evening!

1 Make the glaze. In a small bowl, whisk together the ingredients and pour into a small saucepan. Bring to the boil over a high heat, then reduce to low and simmer for 10–15 minutes or until thickened and syrupy. Stir occasionally to prevent the glaze from hardening while it cooks.

2 Prepare the peaches. Cut each peach into 8 slices, discarding the stone. Set aside. Snip the courgette noodles into 16 pieces each 15cm long. Try to use as much of the courgette that still has its green skin, and reserve the remainder in an airtight container in the fridge for later use.

3 Toss the courgette noodles in a non-stick frying pan over a medium heat to soften slightly, about 2 minutes. Remove the pan from the heat and set aside.

For the glaze
180ml balsamic vinegar
2 tablespoons honey
Salt

For the peaches
2 ripe peaches
2 large courgettes, spiralized with BLADE C OR BLADE D
Cooking spray
16 thin slices of prosciutto
50g Roquefort cheese

(recipe continues)

4 Place a griddle pan over a medium-high heat and spray with cooking spray. When water flicked onto the pan sizzles, add the peaches and sear for 1 minute on each side, until char marks appear.

5 Lay a piece of prosciutto on a clean, flat surface and fold lengthways to create one long strip. Place one peach slice on the left side of the prosciutto. Crumble about 1 teaspoon of Roquefort over the peach and roll the prosciutto from left to right, until it is completely wrapped around the peach slice. Secure with a cocktail stick. Repeat with remaining peach slices.

6 Lay a courgette noodle on a clean, flat surface. Take one wrapped peach and centre it on the courgette. Carefully tie a knot in the courgette around the peach. Place the knotted peaches on a serving plate and lightly crumble over the remaining Roquefort. Drizzle over the balsamic glaze and serve.

Take care not to pull too tightly on the courgette noodle as you tie it around the peaches – the ribbons snap easily. Instead, pull gently and immediately secure with a cocktail stick.

Apple and Kohlrabi Slaw with Lemon-Mint Chia Seed Dressing

GF

VT

MAKES
2 servings

TIME TO PREPARE
30 minutes

NUTRITIONAL INFORMATION
SERVING SIZE: ½ **recipe**
Calories: 323
Fat: 15g
Carbohydrates: 47g
Salt: 0.1g
Protein: 6g
Sugar: 30g

Chia seeds are from a plant that grows mainly in South America; *chia* is the Mayan word for 'strength'. Don't be fooled – they're tiny, but they pack a heavy nutritional punch! They're loaded with fibre, antioxidants, and protein, making them ideal for weight loss and for building a strong immune system. Thanks to their high fibre content, they absorb over ten times their weight in water, becoming gel-like and expanding in your stomach, thus helping you feel fuller. With this dressing drizzled over this dazzling slaw, you'll have a tasty way to reap all the benefits of chia.

1 Make the dressing. Soak the chia seeds in the water for at least 30 minutes or overnight.

2 Whisk the rest of the dressing ingredients in a small bowl. Whisk in the soaked chia seeds.

3 Make the slaw. Combine all the ingredients in a medium serving bowl and toss to mix well. Drizzle the slaw with the dressing and serve immediately.

For a different texture, cut the kohlrabi and apple in half and use blade B to spiralize them. You'll have half-moon slices that will be heartier and easier to serve.

For the dressing
1 tablespoon chia seeds
120ml water
½ tablespoon chopped fresh mint
1 tablespoon honey
60ml lemon juice
1½ tablespoons olive oil

For the slaw
1 apple, spiralized with **BLADE C**
1 kohlrabi, peeled, spiralized with **BLADE C**
30g dried cranberries
4 tablespoons lightly crushed cashews
1 small carrot, peeled and shaved into strips with a vegetable peeler

Beetroot, Goat's Cheese, and Pomegranate Chicory Cups

MAKES
12 hors d'oeuvres

GF

TIME TO PREPARE
20 minutes

TIME TO COOK
5 minutes

NUTRITIONAL INFORMATION
SERVING SIZE: 1 chicory cup with 4 tablespoons of filling
Calories: 69
Fat: 4g
Carbohydrates: 4g
Salt: 0.2g
Protein: 3g
Sugar: 3g

These chicory 'cups' take very little time to make, but they look elegant and festive. Plus, they're packed with superfoods, and the goat's cheese has a creamy sweetness that takes the bite out of the otherwise bitter chicory. Just be prepared to share the recipe – these are a crowd-pleaser!

Try to find the biggest heads of chicory possible so that you'll have large leaves to pack in the filling.

1 In a small bowl, whisk together the vinegar, olive oil, honey, and salt and pepper.

2 Place the beetroot rice in a medium bowl and toss with the goat's cheese, pomegranate seeds, and dressing.

3 Separate the chicory and select 12 large leaves to serve as cups. Fill each leaf with the beetroot mixture, then transfer to a large plate and serve.

2 teaspoons white balsamic vinegar

2 teaspoons olive oil

2 teaspoons honey

Salt and pepper

2 large golden beetroots, peeled, spiralized with **BLADE C**, then riced (see page 25)

60g goat's cheese, crumbled

75g pomegranate seeds

4 large heads chicory

Mango-Avocado Cucumber Spring Rolls with Sriracha-Lime Dipping Sauce

MAKES
6 rolls (12 pieces)

TIME TO PREPARE
15 minutes

NUTRITIONAL INFORMATION
SERVING SIZE: 1 roll
Calories: 116
Fat: 4g
Carbohydrates: 21g
Salt: 1.1g
Protein: 2g
Sugar: 13g

ALSO WORKS WELL WITH
Courgettes • Kohlrabi

My first job out of university was in event and hotel management at a golf club that was a 45-minute drive from where I lived at the time. When I worked on weekends, I'd stop on my way out there at my favourite supermarket and pick up some spring rolls just like these. I'd stuff them into the fridge when I got there, work a full day, and then eat them on my ride home – a fresh, crunchy treat. The combination of sweet mango and mashed avocado is heavenly, especially with the spicy lime dipping sauce. The cucumber noodles add unexpected crunch, too. Here's my at-home version of those spring rolls.

1 In a medium bowl, combine the avocado with salt, pepper, the lime juice, coriander, and mango.

2 Make the dipping sauce. Whisk the ingredients in a medium bowl. Transfer to a serving bowl and place in the fridge to chill until ready to serve.

3 Fill a large bowl with warm water. Working with one piece at a time, submerge a rice paper wrapper in the water for a few seconds just until softened, then lay on a clean, flat surface. Across the centre, leaving about 5cm space on each side, place a layer of the chard, then top with about one-sixth of the avocado mixture, and finish with a handful of cucumber noodles. Fold the uncovered sides inward and then tightly roll up the wrapper lengthways. Repeat with the remaining ingredients and remaining wrappers.

4 Slice each roll in half and pierce each half with a cocktail stick. Serve with the dipping sauce alongside.

1 avocado, mashed

Salt and pepper

1 tablespoon lime juice

1 tablespoon finely chopped fresh coriander

1 small mango, cubed

For the dipping sauce

4 tablespoons soy sauce

2 tablespoons lime juice

2 tablespoons honey

2 tablespoons Sriracha or other hot sauce

Salt and pepper

6 rice paper wrappers for spring rolls

75g rainbow chard or other green, chopped

1 medium cucumber, spiralized with **BLADE C**

SOUPS, STEWS & SALADS

Chicken Carrot Noodle Soup

Ginger Spring Onion Egg Drop Soup

Cajun Beef and Celeriac Chilli

Daikon Ramen with Skirt Steak

Prawn Daikon Pho

Steak and Pear Kale Salad

Caprese Courgette Salad

Avocado-Lime Mason Jar Salad

Green Apple, Kiwi, and Sweetcorn Salad with
Honey-Mint Dressing

Pear, Fontina, and Fig Salad with Honey-Pistachio Dressing

Pickled Onion and Watermelon Salad with Parmesan

Apples with Shaved Asparagus, Gorgonzola, and Pecans

Tomatokeftedes and Cauliflower Tabouleh Salad

Cucumber Noodle Salad with Feta, Rocket, and
Red Wine Vinaigrette

Chicken Carrot Noodle Soup

MAKES
2–3 servings

TIME TO PREPARE
25 minutes

TIME TO COOK
15 minutes

NUTRITIONAL INFORMATION
SERVING SIZE: $^1/_3$ **recipe**
Calories: 212
Fat: 11g
Carbohydrates: 6g
Salt: 2.6g
Protein: 23g
Sugar: 2g

ALSO WORKS WELL WITH
Daikon Radishes •
Kohlrabi • Broccoli
Stems • Celeriac •
Sweet Potatoes •
Butternut Squash

Instead of adding chopped carrots to this classic, why not use the carrots as a substitute for egg noodles? They offer a subtle crunch, which complements the simplicity of the preparation. Everyone needs a little comfort every once in a while, and this soup provides exactly that, without the starch or accompanying bloat. Small changes like this yield big results.

1 Heat the olive oil in a large saucepan over a medium heat. When the oil is shimmering, add the garlic, celery, and onion. Season with salt and pepper and cook, stirring, for 3–5 minutes or until the onion is translucent and the vegetables begin to soften.

2 Add the stock, thyme, oregano, and parsley. Increase the heat to high and bring to the boil, then reduce to low and simmer for 5 minutes. Add the chicken and carrot noodles. Cook for about 5 minutes, or until the noodles soften, and serve.

2 tablespoons olive oil

1½ large garlic cloves, finely chopped

2 celery sticks, halved lengthways and chopped

½ medium white onion, chopped

Salt and pepper

950ml reduced-salt chicken stock

4 thyme sprigs

½ teaspoon dried oregano

1 teaspoon chopped fresh parsley

250–300g shredded rotisserie chicken

1 large carrot, peeled, spiralized with **BLADE A**

If you want to mimic the traditional wide egg noodles, substitute with courgette noodles using blade A. Add them at the very end, cooking for just 2–3 minutes or until *al dente*.

Ginger Spring Onion Egg Drop Soup

MAKES
1 serving

TIME TO PREPARE
10 minutes

TIME TO COOK
15 minutes

NUTRITIONAL INFORMATION
SERVING SIZE: 1 recipe quantity
Calories: 243
Fat: 15g
Carbohydrates: 15g
Salt: 6.4g
Protein: 10g
Sugar: 9g

ALSO WORKS WELL WITH
Daikon Radish •
Kohlrabi

On one of our first dates, Lu brought me to the Momofuku noodle bar, in New York City's East Village. At the time I wasn't eating meat, and everything on the menu seemed to contain crispy pork belly or sausage. Then, my eyes landed on the ginger spring onion noodles. It could've been the giddiness of being with Lu, but I was blown away by how flavourful this simple dish was. Later, I wanted to add some protein to my version, so I turned it into a half egg drop soup, half ginger spring onion noodles. As this recipe shows, every moment is an opportunity to Inspiralize something great.

1 Heat the oil in a large saucepan over a medium heat. When the oil is shimmering, add the ginger and cook for 1 minute, stirring frequently. Increase the heat to high and add the crushed dried chillies, sherry vinegar, soy sauce, stock, and water.

2 Bring the stock to the boil, then add the seaweed. Slowly pour in the egg while rapidly stirring. Add the courgette noodles, spring onions, and pepper, and cook for about 2 minutes or until the noodles are cooked through but still crisp. Transfer to a bowl and serve.

The faster you whisk the egg into the stock, the wispier it will get. If you want larger egg wisps, whisk slowly.

¾ tablespoon rapeseed oil

1 tablespoon finely chopped fresh ginger

¼ teaspoon crushed dried chillies

2 teaspoons sherry vinegar

1 tablespoon reduced-salt soy sauce

480ml reduced-salt vegetable stock

120ml water

3 tablespoons dried seaweed ribbons

1 medium egg, lightly beaten

½ large courgette, spiralized with BLADE C

35g spring onion, green and white parts, chopped

Freshly ground pepper

Cajun Beef and Celeriac Chilli

MAKES
4 servings

GF

P

TIME TO PREPARE
15 minutes

TIME TO COOK
25 minutes

NUTRITIONAL INFORMATION
SERVING SIZE: ¼ **recipe**
Calories: 253
Fat: 10g
Carbohydrates: 15g
Salt: 0.6g
Protein: 27g
Sugar: 7g

ALSO WORKS WELL WITH
Sweet Potatoes •
Butternut Squash •
Swedes

I could eat turkey chilli with brown rice on every rainy, cold day in the autumn. This recipe takes it up a notch, with celeriac rice instead. It offers familiar texture, but also a fresh, earthy taste that helps combat the heaviness of the beef – plus it squeezes extra nutrients into your meal. Save this one for those chilly days when you're craving something filling and warm.

1 Heat the olive oil in large saucepan over a medium heat. When the oil is shimmering, add the onion, garlic, and crushed dried chillies and cook for 30 seconds or until fragrant. Add the beef, breaking it up with a wooden spoon, and cook for 3–5 minutes more, or until browned.

2 Add the celeriac rice, tomatoes, stock, cumin, cayenne, chilli powder, onion powder, oregano, paprika, bay leaf, salt, and pepper, and stir to combine. Cover and cook for 10 minutes, then uncover and continue cooking for 5–10 minutes more or until the chilli is thick and the celeriac has softened.

3 Remove the pan from the heat, discard the bay leaf, then sprinkle with parsley and serve hot.

1 tablespoon olive oil

65g white onion, chopped

1 tablespoon finely chopped garlic

¼ teaspoon crushed dried chillies

450g lean beef mince

1 large celeriac knob, peeled, spiralized with BLADE C, then riced (see page 25)

800g tinned chopped tomatoes, no salt added

120ml reduced-salt beef stock

2 teaspoons ground cumin

½ teaspoon cayenne pepper

½ teaspoon chilli powder

½ teaspoon onion powder

1 teaspoon dried oregano

¼ teaspoon smoked paprika

1 bay leaf

Salt and pepper

1 tablespoon finely chopped fresh parsley

Daikon Ramen with Skirt Steak

MAKES
2 servings

TIME TO PREPARE
10 minutes

TIME TO COOK
20 minutes

NUTRITIONAL INFORMATION
SERVING SIZE: 1/2 **recipe**
Calories: 391
Fat: 26g
Carbohydrates: 11g
Salt: 3.2g
Protein: 28g
Sugar: 6g

ALSO WORKS WELL WITH
Courgette • Turnips •
Kohlrabi • Carrots

This noodle dish has the consistency and flavour profile of ramen noodles without the, well, ramen. Don't get me wrong, I used to eat the instant stuff at uni; it's salty and addictively tasty, but has the nutritional value of cardboard. Whenever you eat, it's important to ask yourself, 'Is this food going to make me feel good? Is it what my body needs to get me through the day?' If the answer is no, ditch it. By swapping the daikon here, you're replacing the empty noodles with a root vegetable that's rich in vitamin C and low in calories and carbohydrates. If I had only known at university!

1 Slice the thick white stems off the pak choi and then chop the green leaves in half.

2 Coat the steak with hoisin sauce and generously season with salt and pepper. Heat a large frying pan over a medium heat and add the olive oil. When the oil is shimmering, add the steak and cook for 2–3 minutes on each side or until it reaches your desired doneness; keep in mind that the steak will cook slightly more once it is removed from the heat. Set the steak on a chopping board.

3 Place a large pot over a medium heat and add the vegetable oil. When the oil is shimmering, add the garlic, ginger, and spring onions. Cook for 30 seconds or until fragrant, then add the mushrooms and the pak choi. Cook for 3–4 minutes or until the mushrooms are softened.

1 bunch pak choi

115g boneless skirt steak

1 tablespoon hoisin sauce

Salt and pepper

1 tablespoon olive oil

1 tablespoon vegetable oil

1 teaspoon finely chopped garlic

1/2 teaspoon finely chopped fresh ginger

25g spring onions, green and white parts, sliced

100g shiitake mushrooms

480ml reduced-salt vegetable stock

240ml water

2 teaspoons reduced-salt soy sauce

1 medium daikon radish, peeled, spiralized with BLADE C

2 hard-boiled eggs, halved

4 Add the stock, water, and soy sauce. Increase the heat to high and bring to the boil. Reduce the heat to low, and add the daikon noodles. Cook for 2 minutes or until the noodles are *al dente*.

5 Thinly slice the skirt steak against the grain. Serve the ramen in portions topped with steak slices and the egg halves.

Prawn Daikon Pho

MAKES
2 servings

GF

TIME TO PREPARE
20 minutes

TIME TO COOK
15 minutes

NUTRITIONAL INFORMATION
SERVING SIZE: ¹/₂ recipe
Calories: 87
Fat: 1 g
Carbohydrates: 11g
Salt: 5.4g
Protein: 9g
Sugar: 4g

ALSO WORKS WELL WITH
Courgette • Kohlrabi

One weekend I was out walking and I saw a new restaurant called Pho-nomenal. (Let's just say that when you start with the 'pho' jokes, you can't stop. Pho-gettabout it. Pho-shizzle. Pho real.) Pho – pronounced 'fuh' – is a flavourful Vietnamese street food that varies in sweetness and noodle type. I've adapted and simplified the traditional dish by replacing the rice noodles with daikon noodles for a lighter, spicier version.

1 Place a large soup pot over a medium heat and add the stock, water, fish sauce, lime juice, coriander, and ginger. Season with salt and pepper, increase the heat to high, bring to the boil, and add the prawns. Reduce the heat to medium-low and cook at a strong simmer for about 5 minutes, or until prawns are cooked through and opaque.

2 Add the daikon noodles and coriander, stir to combine, and cook for about 2 minutes more, until the daikon noodles are softened.

3 Serve the pho hot, garnished with the spring onions, jalapeños, onion slices, and hot sauce, if desired.

This pho base can be customized to your preference by using beef, chicken, or tofu – all common pho proteins.

700ml reduced-salt vegetable stock

480ml water

2 teaspoons Vietnamese or Thai fish sauce

3 tablespoons fresh lime juice

1 teaspoon ground coriander

1 teaspoon finely chopped fresh ginger

Salt and pepper

12 small prawns, peeled and deveined, defrosted if frozen

1 large daikon radish, peeled, spiralized with BLADE C

5–10g whole coriander leaves

2–3 spring onions, green and white parts, chopped

2 small jalapeño peppers (or 1 large), deseeded and thinly sliced crossways

2 thin slices white onion

Sriracha or other hot sauce (optional)

Steak and Pear Kale Salad

MAKES
2 servings

GF

TIME TO PREPARE
20 minutes

TIME TO COOK
10 minutes

NUTRITIONAL INFORMATION
SERVING SIZE: $1/2$ **recipe**
Calories: 525
Fat: 39g
Carbohydrates: 28g
Salt: 1.2g
Protein: 20g
Sugar: 6g

ALSO WORKS WELL WITH
Apples

When I first started putting meat back into my diet after my vegan years, the only way I could stomach red meat was in a salad. New to cooking meat, I spent countless nights in my kitchen, searing steak until it was cooked to my preference: well done with the slightest hint of pink. I would flip the steaks, slice them open, and find that they were either underdone or way too firm. Luckily, even if the steak didn't turn out well, the salad beneath it was prepared to perfection. But finally I mastered the art. This kale salad enhances the flavour of the steak atop it, and will tantalize your taste buds with every crunchy forkful.

1 Prepare the salad. Whisk the honey, oil, vinegar, salt and pepper, mustard, shallot, and water in a large bowl. Add the kale, toss to combine, and set in the fridge to soften.

2 Make the steak. Pat the steak dry and season generously with salt and pepper on both sides. Heat a cast-iron frying pan over a medium-high heat and add the olive oil. When the oil is shimmering, add the steak and cook 3–4 minutes per side. Remove the steak from the heat and allow it to rest for 5 minutes. Cut the meat against the grain into thin slices.

3 Add the pear noodles to the dressed kale and mix well. Place the salad on plates and top with steak slices, then crumble on the blue cheese.

If you don't like blue cheese, substitute with flakes or shavings of Parmesan, or just omit it altogether.

For the salad
2 teaspoons honey
3 tablespoons olive oil
2 tablespoons red wine vinegar
Salt and pepper
2 teaspoons Dijon mustard
1 shallot, finely chopped
1 tablespoon water
100g curly kale, chopped

For the steak
115g boneless beef steak (sirloin or fillet)
Salt and pepper
1 tablespoon olive oil
1 large firm pear, spiralized with BLADE C
40g blue cheese, crumbled

Caprese Courgette Salad

MAKES
2–3 servings

GF

TIME TO PREPARE
20 minutes

VT

NUTRITIONAL INFORMATION
SERVING SIZE: ¹/₃ **recipe**
Calories: 216
Fat: 17g
Carbohydrates: 7g
Salt: 0.1g
Protein: 9g
Sugar: 5g

Thinking back to those late-afternoon dinners at my grandparents' house in the summer, I can't recall a single time when my grandfather didn't make a *caprese* salad. This traditional Italian dish is defined by the freshness of the tomatoes and basil and the quality of the olive oil and mozzarella. When you hit all of those points, the salad can't be anything but extraordinary. Balsamic vinegar and lemon juice transform the basics into a perfect salad for a summer evening.

1 Place the courgettes and tomatoes in a large bowl.

2 Make the marinade. Pulse the ingredients in a food processor until the garlic is smooth.

3 Pour the marinade over the courgette noodles and tomatoes, and toss to combine. Place in the fridge to marinate for at least 10 minutes.

4 Add the mozzarella and basil to the courgette noodles, toss to combine, and serve.

2 medium courgettes, spiralized with
BLADE A, then noodles trimmed to
12.5cm or less
300g cherry tomatoes, halved

For the marinade
1 tablespoon lemon juice
3 tablespoons balsamic vinegar
2 tablespoons olive oil
1 medium garlic clove, finely chopped
Salt and pepper

12 small mozzarella balls, halved
15g fresh basil leaves, thinly sliced

The longer the courgette marinates, the more intense the flavours will be, so don't be afraid to prepare this salad in advance.

Avocado-Lime Mason Jar Salad

MAKES
4 servings

GF

TIME TO PREPARE
15 minutes

TIME TO COOK
15 minutes

NUTRITIONAL INFORMATION
SERVING SIZE: 1 jar
Calories: 331
Fat: 24g
Carbohydrates: 18g
Salt: 0.2g
Protein: 16g
Sugar: 6g

ALSO WORKS WELL WITH
Kohlrabi • Carrots •
Beetroot

If you're not eating dairy, using avocado to thicken your dressings for pasta salads is a handy trick. Avocados are not only tasty but also a powerful source of healthy monosaturated fat, which is especially important in a low-carb diet. This salad is full of protein and Mexican-inspired flavour. The olives, coriander, and lime juice add tanginess and freshness to the courgette noodles. It's appropriate for a summertime barbecue or a lean weeknight meal. You'll need four 450g preserving jars. Just pour the jars into bowls when you're ready to eat!

1 Heat the olive oil in a large non-stick frying pan over a medium heat. When the oil is shimmering, add the chicken and season with salt and pepper. Cook for 6–8 minutes until lightly browned on the outside and no longer pink on the inside.

2 Place the sweetcorn in a medium saucepan over a high heat, cover with water, and add a pinch of salt. Bring to the boil and cook for 2–3 minutes, or until the sweetcorn is easily pierced with a fork. Drain and, when cooled to the touch, slice the kernels off the cobs.

3 Make the dressing. Combine the coriander, garlic, salt and pepper, olive oil, lime juice, and avocado in a food processor and pulse until creamy. One tablespoon at a time, add some room-temperature water until the dressing reaches the desired consistency, pulsing after every addition.

1 tablespoon olive oil

225g boneless chicken,
   cut into 1cm dice

Salt and pepper

2 ears of sweetcorn, husked and silks
   removed

For the dressing

2–3 tablespoons chopped fresh
   coriander

1 medium garlic clove, finely chopped

Salt and pepper

3 tablespoons olive oil

2 tablespoons lime juice

1 avocado, cubed

½ large red pepper, diced

85g black olives, halved and pitted

3 medium courgettes, spiralized
   with **BLADE C**

4 Place one-quarter of the dressing at the bottom of four 450g preserving jars and add a serving of chicken. Then layer in the peppers, olives, and the sweetcorn kernels. Finally, top each jar with some of the courgette noodles. Place tops on the jars and refrigerate for up to 1 day or serve at room temperature within 3 hours.

Avocado browns quickly, so if you're making this dish in advance, prepare everything except the dressing. Assemble the dressing right before serving.

Green Apple, Kiwi, and Sweetcorn Salad with Honey-Mint Dressing

MAKES
3 servings

TIME TO PREPARE
15 minutes

TIME TO COOK
10 minutes

NUTRITIONAL INFORMATION
SERVING SIZE: $^1/_3$ **recipe**
Calories: 193
Fat: 5g
Carbohydrates: 32g
Salt: 0g
Protein: 3g
Sugar: 24g

What makes this particular salad special is the honey-mint dressing – you'll be licking the bowl clean afterwards. The combination of kiwi and sweetcorn offers a crunchy sweetness that's amplified by the mint dressing. This salad pairs especially well with freshly grilled fish.

1 Place the sweetcorn in a medium saucepan over a high heat, cover with water, and add a pinch of salt. Bring to the boil and cook for 2 minutes or until the sweetcorn is easily pierced with a fork. Drain and let cool, then slice the kernels off the cob.

2 Make the dressing. Whisk together the mint, olive oil, water, honey, vinegar, lime juice, and salt and pepper in a large bowl.

3 Add the sweetcorn kernels, the apple, kiwis, and lettuce to the bowl with the dressing. Toss to combine thoroughly, then transfer to a serving bowl.

1 large ear sweetcorn, husked and silks removed

For the dressing
1 tablespoon chopped fresh mint

1 tablespoon olive oil

1 tablespoon water

2 tablespoons honey

2 tablespoons white balsamic vinegar

2 teaspoons lime juice

Salt and pepper

1 medium green apple, peeled, spiralized with **BLADE C**

3 kiwi fruits, peeled and cubed

1 round lettuce, roughly chopped

If you make this salad in advance, combine all the ingredients except the lettuce. Allow the salad to sit for a few hours so the apple softens as it absorbs the dressing.

Pear, Fontina, and Fig Salad with Honey-Pistachio Dressing

MAKES
3–4 servings

GF

TIME TO PREPARE
20 minutes

VT

NUTRITIONAL INFORMATION
SERVING SIZE: ¼ **recipe**
Calories: 273
Fat: 16g
Carbohydrates: 29g
Salt: 0.6g
Protein: 7g
Sugar: 21g

ALSO WORKS WELL WITH
Apples

Lu and I have an ongoing debate about which of our favourite local restaurants has the best cheese board. We both love having a good charcuterie and cheese board on Friday night, after a long week. I wanted to re-create those flavours in a recipe. With its boldness, this salad can be a stand-alone meal or it can be served alongside a juicy steak or grilled chicken breast.

1 Make the dressing. Pulse the ingredients in a food processor until fully combined.

2 Prepare the salad. Combine the pear noodles, chard, and figs in a large bowl.

3 Toss the noodles with the dressing and serve, topped with fontina strips and pistachios.

For the dressing
120ml balsamic vinegar

2 tablespoons olive oil

2 tablespoons honey

Black pepper

For the salad
2 firm pears, spiralized with BLADE C

225g chard, shredded (see Tip)

70g quartered fresh figs

About 20 pieces fontina cheese, in 5mm-thick matchsticks

30g roasted and salted pistachios

To shred the chard, cut away the tough white stems. Roll up the leafy parts like a cigar and cut into 3mm slices. When you're finished, the chard will be shredded. This trick works for basil, too!

Pickled Onion and Watermelon Salad with Parmesan

MAKES
3 servings

GF **VT**

TIME TO PREPARE
25 minutes

TIME TO COOK
10 minutes

NUTRITIONAL INFORMATION
SERVING SIZE: $^1/_3$ **recipe**
Calories: 119
Fat: 3g
Carbohydrates: 21g
Salt: 0g
Protein: 3g
Sugar: 17g

There's nothing like sitting outside, watching the summer sun go down, and sipping a glass of wine or iced tea. What could possibly make the scene better? A tasty snack! This refreshing salad is sure to hit the spot. The Parmesan adds hard texture and provides a kick of flavour. Most importantly, the pickled onions are long and twirly – fun to eat and an impressive presentation!

1 In a medium bowl, combine the vinegar, onion noodles, honey, and salt. Let marinate in the fridge for 15–20 minutes.

2 Combine the watermelon and mint in a large bowl. Add the pickled onion noodles and toss. Transfer to a serving bowl and top with the Parmesan.

60ml red wine vinegar

1 small red onion, peeled, spiralized with **BLADE A**

1 tablespoon honey

Pinch of salt

450g watermelon, cubed

1 tablespoon fresh mint leaves

Shavings of Parmesan

Apples with Shaved Asparagus, Gorgonzola, and Pecans

MAKES
2 servings

TIME TO PREPARE
15 minutes

NUTRITIONAL INFORMATION
SERVING SIZE: $^1/_2$ **recipe**
Calories: 316
Fat: 24g
Carbohydrates: 21g
Salt: 0.7g
Protein: 7g
Sugar: 16g

Sometimes you just need a salad. Before I left corporate life, I'd buy one every day for lunch. But the ingredients were so predictable – raw or steamed veggies, sliced fruits, diced proteins. Now you can keep your salads interesting by adding fruit noodles! This salad tastes gourmet and looks fancy, too, with its rich cheese, crunchy pecans, and dainty shaved asparagus. Every bite is exciting!

1 Make the dressing. Whisk the ingredients in a medium bowl. Taste and adjust the seasoning.

2 Prepare the salad. Using a vegetable peeler, thinly shave each asparagus spear. In a large bowl, combine the shaved asparagus, watercress, pecans, and apple noodles.

3 Drizzle with the vinaigrette, toss to combine, and serve topped with the Gorgonzola.

For the dressing
1 tablespoon honey
1 tablespoon olive oil
1 tablespoon red wine vinegar
2 teaspoons Dijon mustard
1 tablespoon water
1 tablespoon finely chopped shallot
Salt and pepper

For the salad
10 large asparagus spears, tough ends snapped off
50g watercress
35g roughly chopped pecans
1 apple, spiralized with **BLADE C**
30g Gorgonzola cheese, crumbled

For a protein boost, add thinly sliced steak, grilled chicken, or quinoa.

Tomatokeftedes and Cauliflower Tabouleh Salad

MAKES
2–3 servings

GF

VT

TIME TO PREPARE
35 minutes

TIME TO COOK
20 minutes

NUTRITIONAL INFORMATION
SERVING SIZE: 1/3 **recipe**
Calories: 170
Fat: 6g
Carbohydrates: 24g
Salt: 0.8g
Protein: 9g
Sugar: 7g

ALSO WORKS WELL WITH
Courgettes • Kohlrabi

The first getaway trip Lu and I took together as a couple was to Santorini and Mykonos, in Greece. When we arrived at our hotel on Santorini, it was late at night, but we were ravenous from almost 20 hours of travelling. We dropped our bags and walked a few minutes to a small nearby restaurant and asked for "anything Santorinian". The waitress brought us *tomatokeftedes* – fried tomato balls. I don't know if it was the exhaustion or the excitement, but I will never forget that first bite. Of course, we devoured them and ordered more. For the rest of our stay on Santorini we never ate at a restaurant without ordering their *tomatokeftedes*. These healthy tomato balls are my way of bringing a bit of Santorini to you.

For the tomatokeftedes
Cooking spray

170g small cherry tomatoes, chopped

70g spring onions, green and white parts, chopped

1 tablespoon warm water

1 tablespoon chopped fresh mint

¼ teaspoon dried oregano

30g wholemeal or chickpea flour

20g pecorino romano cheese, grated

Salt and pepper

For the tabouleh
1 large seedless cucumber, spiralized with **BLADE C**

75g cauliflower florets

60g red onion, finely chopped

3 tablespoons chopped fresh flat-leaf parsley

1 tablespoon chopped fresh mint

Salt and pepper

3 tablespoons lemon juice

Zest of half a lemon

For the tzatziki
55g natural 0% fat Greek yogurt

1 medium garlic clove, finely chopped

¼ tablespoon olive oil

¼ tablespoon red wine vinegar

½ tablespoon chopped fresh dill

¾ tablespoon lemon juice

Salt and pepper

(recipe continues)

1 Preheat the oven to 200°C/400°F. Line a baking sheet with parchment paper and coat the paper with cooking spray.

2 Make the *tomatokeftedes*. In a large bowl, add all the ingredients. Using your hands to partially crush the tomatoes, combine the ingredients until the mixture is thick and sticky. (If needed, add more flour and/or water.) Form *tomatokeftedes* about the size of a golf ball; you should have about 6. Place them on the baking sheet and press down slightly to form patties. Bake for 10 minutes, flip them over, and bake for another 10–15 minutes or until browned on the outside and firm.

3 Make the tabouleh. Pat dry the cucumber noodles to remove moisture. Pulse the cauliflower florets in a food processor until rice-like. Add the onion, parsley, mint, salt and pepper, lemon juice, and zest to the food processor and pulse until well combined.

4 Prepare the tzatziki. Whisk the ingredients in a medium bowl.

5 Assemble the meal. Combine the cucumber noodles and the tabouleh mixture in a large bowl and toss to blend well. Divide into serving bowls and top with hot tomato balls. Drizzle over the tzatziki sauce and serve.

Cucumber Noodle Salad with Feta, Rocket, and Red Wine Vinaigrette

MAKES
2 servings

TIME TO PREPARE
15 minutes

NUTRITIONAL INFORMATION
SERVING SIZE: $^1/_2$ **recipe**
Calories: 222
Fat: 18g
Carbohydrates: 14g
Salt: 0.5g
Protein: 4g
Sugar: 8g

This fresh cucumber noodle salad will quickly become a favourite for every occasion. Besides looking effortlessly gorgeous, it can rise to any occasion: add some protein and make a meal out of it; serve it at a barbecue to complement grilled meats and fish; or start a meal with it to spike the palate. The cucumber noodles are crunchy and elegant, and they soak up the dressing better than greens would.

1 Make the vinaigrette. In a medium bowl, whisk the ingredients together.

2 Prepare the salad. Pat the cucumber noodles dry with kitchen paper to remove moisture. Transfer to a large bowl and add the rocket and onion noodles, then toss to combine.

3 Pour the vinaigrette on top, tossing to coat the vegetables. Add the feta, lightly toss, and transfer to a serving bowl or plate.

For the vinaigrette
2 tablespoons olive oil
3 tablespoons red wine vinegar
1 tablespoon lemon juice
½ teaspoon dried oregano
Salt and pepper
1 teaspoon honey

For the salad
1 large cucumber, spiralized with BLADE A
40g baby rocket
½ red onion, spiralized with BLADE C
30g feta cheese, crumbled

If you're making this as a full meal, spiralize half a cucumber and half a courgette (instead of 1 full cucumber) for a heartier dish.

Italian Courgette Pasta Salad

MAKES
3–4 servings

TIME TO PREPARE
15 minutes

NUTRITIONAL INFORMATION
SERVING SIZE: 1/4 **recipe**
Calories: 214
Fat: 16g
Carbohydrates: 10g
Salt: 1g
Protein: 8g
Sugar: 3g

When Lu's mother came to New Jersey to meet my family, I threw a dinner party. I wasn't nervous about their meeting, but I was nervous about what to cook! I wanted to serve something that really reflected me, my Italian-American background, and my healthy-kitchen skills. I decided on this classic pasta salad – just without the pasta. My sister's boyfriend, who typically doesn't like courgettes or anything else labelled 'good for you', practically licked his plate clean.

1 Prepare the salad. Slice the courgettes in half lengthways and then spiralize using blade B. In a large bowl, combine the courgette noodles with the artichoke hearts, tomatoes, provolone, salami, red onion, and black olives.

2 Make the dressing. Whisk the ingredients in a small bowl.

3 Pour the dressing over the pasta salad and toss to combine. Refrigerate for at least 15 minutes until the dressing begins to soften the courgettes. Serve chilled.

The longer this pasta salad marinates in the fridge, the deeper the flavours get and the softer the courgette becomes. If possible, let it sit overnight. Shake it up just before serving.

2 medium courgettes

3 tinned artichoke hearts, drained and patted dry

6 cherry tomatoes, halved

60g provolone cheese, cubed

85g salami, diced

1/2 small red onion, thinly sliced

40g pitted black olives, quartered

For the dressing

3 tablespoons red wine vinegar

2 tablespoons olive oil

60ml lemon juice

1/2 teaspoon dried oregano

1/2 teaspoon dried parsley

1/2 teaspoon dried basil

1/4 teaspoon crushed dried chillies

Salt and pepper

SANDWICHES, WRAPS & MORE

Tilapia Tostadas with Tomato-Sweetcorn Salsa

MAKES
3 large tostadas

GF

TIME TO PREPARE
20 minutes

TIME TO COOK
25 minutes

NUTRITIONAL INFORMATION
SERVING SIZE: **1 plantain tostada with 85g of tilapia**
Calories: 532
Fat: 9g
Carbohydrates: 78g
Salt: 0.3g
Protein: 41g
Sugar: 20g

Top a traditional tostada with anything and it'll taste good – but it won't leave you feeling good. Mexican tostadas are fried corn tortillas, but this Inspiralized version is baked and is made with plantain rice. By binding the rice with coconut flakes, the mixture hardens during baking and creates a tostada base with a hint of sweetness and the right amount of crunch. The spicy tilapia pairs well with the refreshing tomato-sweetcorn salsa. This recipe will turn your taco night into plantain tostada night!

Cooking spray

1 ear of sweetcorn, shucked and silks removed

2 large medium-ripe plantains, peeled, spiralized with BLADE C, then riced (see page 25)

1 medium egg and 1 egg white, lightly beaten

2 tablespoons unsweetened coconut flakes

Salt and pepper

3 (85g) pieces of tilapia fillet

1 teaspoon chilli powder

1 lime, cut into 3 thick slices

For the salsa

40g red onion, diced

80g deseeded ripe tomatoes, diced

1 tablespoon fresh lime juice

Salt and pepper

400g tinned black beans, rinsed and drained

2 tablespoons water

1 tablespoon fresh lime juice

1 tablespoon finely chopped fresh coriander

55g cos lettuce, shredded

1 tablespoon crumbled *queso fresco* or mild feta cheese

1 Preheat the oven to 200°C/400°F. Line two baking sheets with parchment paper and lightly coat with cooking spray.

2 Place the sweetcorn in a medium saucepan and cover with salted water. Bring to the boil over a high heat and cook for 2–3 minutes or until easily pierced with a fork. When cool to the touch, slice the kernels off into a small bowl.

3 In a medium bowl, combine the plantain rice with the beaten eggs and coconut flakes. Toss to coat, and season with salt and pepper. Using your hands, place one-third of the plantain mixture on one of the prepared baking sheets. Flatten and round out the edges to make it tostada shaped. Repeat with the remaining mixture, placing all three tostadas on the same baking sheet. Bake for 15–17 minutes until solid.

4 Season the tilapia with the chilli powder, salt, and pepper. Squeeze a lime slice over each, transfer to the remaining prepared baking sheet, and bake for 13–15 minutes alongside the tostadas.

You can turn this tostada into a pliable soft taco by baking it for only 13–15 minutes.

5 Prepare the salsa. Mix all the ingredients in a medium bowl. Add the sweetcorn kernels.

6 Heat the beans in a small saucepan with the water and lime juice until warmed through. Transfer to a food processor, add the coriander, and pulse until the mixture becomes pasty but still has some chunks.

7 Assemble the tostadas. Smear each tostada with the bean mixture and top with shredded lettuce. Layer on the tilapia, breaking the pieces into chunks. Add the salsa and the *queso fresco*, then serve immediately.

Tuna Parsnip Portobello Melts

MAKES
2 melts

GF

TIME TO PREPARE
15 minutes

TIME TO COOK
25 minutes

NUTRITIONAL INFORMATION
SERVING SIZE:
1 portobello melt with
1 slice of cheese
Calories: 269
Fat: 13g
Carbohydrates: 24g
Salt: 1.4g
Protein: 18g
Sugar: 4g

ALSO WORKS WELL WITH
Sweet Potatoes •
Swedes • Potatoes

My Grandma Ida loves tuna salad with biscuits. I can't even begin to count the number of times she came to my parents' house and my mother brought out the tuna with mayo and a stack of saltine crackers. Eventually, even though Grandma Ida didn't, *I* graduated to tuna melts. Now I use 'fayonnaise' to make my tuna melts with 0% fat Greek yogurt, which has more zing and doesn't pack on the processed fat. These melts require a little extra time, but your taste buds will thank you. The warm portobello mushrooms and the nutty parsnip noodles are reason enough to love them – but if you need more reasons, there is also the melted provolone, a healthier tuna salad, and juicy tomatoes. These melts are best eaten with a knife and fork, since delicious can sometimes be a little messy!

For the mushrooms
- 2 large portobello mushroom caps, gills and stem end scooped out
- 1 tablespoon olive oil, plus 2 tablespoons for brushing
- Salt and pepper
- 1 medium garlic clove, finely chopped
- Pinch of crushed dried chillies
- 1 large parsnip, peeled, spiralized with **BLADE C**

For the tuna fayonnaise
- 3 tablespoons natural 0% fat Greek yogurt
- 1 teaspoon Dijon mustard
- ¼ teaspoon garlic powder
- Salt and pepper
- 1 tablespoon fresh lemon juice
- 140g tinned solid white albacore tuna or yellowfin tuna in water, drained

For the melts
- 4 thin tomato slices
- 2 slices provolone cheese
- 1 tablespoon chopped chives

1 Preheat the oven to 200°C/400°F. Line a baking sheet with aluminium foil.

2 Prepare the mushrooms. Spread the portobello caps evenly on the baking sheet, gill side up. Brush both sides with olive oil and season with salt and pepper. Bake for 10 minutes or until slightly wilted.

3 Place a large frying pan over a medium heat and add the tablespoon of olive oil. When the oil is shimmering, add the garlic and crushed dried chillies, and cook for 30 seconds or until fragrant. Add the parsnip noodles and season with salt and pepper. Cover and cook for 5 minutes, uncovering and tossing occasionally, until the parsnip noodles are *al dente*. Remove from the heat.

4 Make the tuna fayonnaise. Combine the yogurt, mustard, garlic powder, salt and pepper, and lemon juice in a medium bowl. Fold in the tuna, breaking it up, and check the seasonings.

5 Assemble the melts. Remove the baking sheet from the oven, but keep the oven on. Pat the roasted mushrooms as dry as possible. In the centre of each cap place half the parsnip noodles. Top each with half the tuna mixture, then with 2 tomato slices. Place a slice of provolone on each cap and return the baking sheet to the oven to bake the mushrooms for 5 minutes more, or until the cheese is melted. Sprinkle the mushroom melts with chives and serve.

Want to barbecue these? Even better! Sear the portobello mushrooms on the grill first.

Beetroot Rice Nori Rolls with Chipotle-Teriyaki Sauce

MAKES
2 rolls (12 pieces)

TIME TO PREPARE
25 minutes

NUTRITIONAL INFORMATION
SERVING SIZE: **1 roll
(6 pieces) + half the
dipping sauce**
Calories: 290
Fat: 18g
Carbohydrates: 32g
Salt: 3.1g
Protein: 6g
Sugar: 28g

ALSO WORKS WELL WITH
Courgettes • Kohlrabi •
Carrots

Is the answer ever *no* to the question, 'Want to grab some sushi tonight?' Sushi is gorgeous and colourful, and it comes in so many different flavour combinations, but the sticky rice can pack a high calorie, sugar, and carbohydrate count, leaving you feeling heavy afterwards. So ditch the pricey sushi joint and make your own, using spiralized vegetable rice! With beetroot rice, you're adding nutrients and colour while you subtract the not-so-good-for-you stuff. That equation sounds Inspiralized to me.

1 Make the sauce. Pulse the ingredients in a food processor or high-speed blender until creamy. Season with salt and pepper to taste.

2 Make the rolls. Working with one sheet at a time, place a nori sheet on a clean, dry surface. Smear the avocado all over, covering completely in a thin layer. Sprinkle the beetroot rice evenly over, using the back of a spoon to press gently into the avocado. Place the cucumber noodles on the bottom quarter of the sheet.

3 Rolling away from your body, roll the nori and rice over the cucumber noodles, adding pressure and compressing the roll with your fingers so that it is tightly formed. Continue until nori is entirely rolled. Repeat for the second nori sheet.

4 Using a sharp knife, slice each roll into 6 pieces. Drizzle the sauce over the pieces or serve it alongside for dipping.

For the sauce
60ml reduced-salt soy sauce
2 tablespoons honey
½ teaspoon finely chopped fresh ginger
1 tablespoon toasted sesame oil
1 chipotle chilli in adobo sauce, with 1 teaspoon sauce
1 teaspoon finely chopped garlic
Salt and pepper

For the nori rolls
2 sheets nori (dried seaweed)
1 avocado, mashed
1 medium beetroot, peeled, spiralized with BLADE C OR BLADE D, then riced (see page 25)
½ seedless cucumber, spiralized with BLADE C OR BLADE D

It's essential that your avocado mash be completely smooth. If this layer is too thick or chunky, the sushi will be too difficult to roll and will fall apart.

Chicken Banh Mi with Sriracha Greek Yogurt

MAKES
4 sandwiches

TIME TO PREPARE
20 minutes

TIME TO COOK
15 minutes

NUTRITIONAL INFORMATION
SERVING SIZE: **1 sandwich**
Calories: 260
Fat: 6g
Carbohydrates: 27g
Salt: 1.5g
Protein: 24g
Sugar: 23g

ALSO WORKS WELL WITH
Courgettes • Onions

One of my simplest tricks is to eat sandwiches open-faced – not only for health reasons but also for greater flavour! If you've ever had a banh mi sandwich, you know the bun can easily overpower the delicious pickled vegetable filling in this classic Vietnamese street food. Here, I've replaced the bun with a red pepper, which not only offers a hydrating crunch but also is a low-calorie, low-carbohydrate vehicle for showcasing what you came for: the pickled (spiralized) vegetables, Asian marinated chicken, and a high-protein Sriracha spread made with 0% fat Greek yogurt.

For the pickled vegetables

60ml rice vinegar

2 tablespoons honey

½ teaspoon salt

1 small daikon radish, peeled, spiralized with **BLADE C OR BLADE D**

1 medium carrot, peeled, spiralized with **BLADE C OR BLADE D**

1 medium cucumber, spiralized with **BLADE C OR BLADE D**

For the chicken

1 tablespoon extra-virgin olive oil

1 tablespoon reduced-salt soy sauce

1 tablespoon hoisin sauce

1 tablespoon fresh lime juice

1 teaspoon honey

340–450g boneless chicken breast, cut into strips

For the Sriracha yogurt

5 tablespoons natural 0% fat Greek yogurt

1 tablespoon Sriracha or other hot sauce

For the sandwiches

2 large red peppers

5g fresh coriander leaves

(recipe continues)

1 Pickle the vegetables. Whisk together the vinegar, honey, and salt in a medium bowl. Add the daikon radish, carrot, and cucumber noodles; toss to coat well, then marinate in the fridge until ready to assemble the sandwiches, tossing every 5 minutes.

2 Prepare the chicken. Whisk together the olive oil, soy sauce, hoisin sauce, lime juice, and honey in a shallow dish. Add the chicken and turn to coat. Heat a large griddle pan over a medium heat. When a bit of water flicked onto the pan sizzles, add the chicken and sear for 10 minutes, flipping over halfway through, until no longer pink. Cut into thin slices.

3 Make the Sriracha yogurt. In a small bowl, whisk the ingredients together.

4 Assemble the sandwiches. Slice the tops off both peppers, remove and discard the seeds and white flesh, and halve them vertically to yield four sandwich 'bottoms'. Lay out the pepper pieces with the insides facing up. Spread on the Sriracha mayo, then layer on the chicken and top with the pickled vegetables. Drizzle the tops with extra yogurt, if desired, and garnish with the coriander.

Spring Greens Hummous Wraps with Golden Beetroot and Sprouts

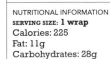

MAKES
2 wraps

TIME TO PREPARE
15 minutes

TIME TO COOK
10 minutes

NUTRITIONAL INFORMATION
SERVING SIZE: 1 wrap
Calories: 225
Fat: 11g
Carbohydrates: 28g
Salt: 0.4g
Protein: 7g
Sugar: 4g

ALSO WORKS WELL WITH
Courgettes •
Cucumbers • Carrots

Spring greens are nature's sandwich wrap. These large cabbage-family plants yield giant leaves that are perfect for holding ingredients. Here, the warm roasted golden beetroot practically melts into the creamy avocado and hummous, while the alfalfa sprouts add a great texture. This spring greens wrap is quick to make and it packs a big nutritional punch – perfect for fuelling up on busy days of blogging and cooking. You can substitute large kale leaves if you can't find spring greens.

1 Preheat the oven to 200°C/400°F. Line a baking sheet with parchment paper. Spread the beetroot noodles in an even layer and lightly coat with olive oil cooking spray. Season with salt and pepper. Roast for 10 minutes or until softened, tossing halfway through.

2 Lay the spring greens on a clean, dry surface. Spread the centre of each leaf with about half the hummous, leaving a 2.5–4cm border.

3 Divide the beetroot noodles between the leaves, atop the hummous. Add 2 slices of avocado to each leaf, then top with alfalfa sprouts. Fold the sides in and roll the leaves up like a burrito. Slice each in half, and secure with cocktail sticks before serving.

1 large golden beetroot, peeled, spiralized with **BLADE C**

Olive oil cooking spray

Salt and pepper

2 large spring green or kale leaves, thick centre stems removed as much as possible

100g hummous

½ avocado, quartered

75g alfalfa sprouts

Spicy Prawn Lettuce Wraps with Coconut-Lime Turnip Rice

MAKES
8–10 wraps

GF

P

TIME TO PREPARE
15 minutes

TIME TO COOK
15 minutes

NUTRITIONAL INFORMATION
SERVING SIZE: 1 lettuce wrap + 4 tablespoons of filling
Calories: 62
Fat: 3g
Carbohydrates: 2g
Salt: 0.1g
Protein: 5g
Sugar: 2g

ALSO WORKS WELL WITH
Carrots • Beetroot • Kohlrabi

Lettuce wraps are life-changing. They are a cleaner, healthier alternative to a processed tortilla or wrap, and they are versatile. Here, we have a Latin American vibe, with the chilli powder, coconut, and lime. Each lettuce wrap has a breezy Caribbean taste, perfectly suited for noshing at the beach – or at least for closing your eyes and pretending that's where you are!

1 Marinate the prawns. Combine the prawns, spices, salt, pepper, and olive oil in a bowl and toss to coat evenly. Place in the fridge to chill while you continue cooking.

2 Prepare the turnip rice. Heat the olive oil in a medium non-stick frying pan over a medium heat. When the oil is shimmering, add the garlic and onion. Cook for 2–3 minutes or until the onion is translucent. Add the turnip rice, lime juice, and coconut flakes and stir to combine. Cover the frying pan and cook for 5 minutes, stirring occasionally, until the turnip rice is cooked through and no longer crunchy.

3 Place a large non-stick frying pan over a medium heat. When a little water flicked onto the frying pan sizzles, add the marinated prawns. Cook for 2–3 minutes per side, until opaque and pink.

For the prawns
225g raw small prawns, peeled and deveined
1 teaspoon chilli powder
½ teaspoon smoked paprika
Salt and pepper
1 tablespoon olive oil

For the turnip rice
1 tablespoon extra-virgin olive oil
1 tablespoon finely chopped garlic
½ white onion, sliced into thin strips
1 medium turnip, peeled, spiralized with **BLADE C**, then riced (see page 25) and drained
Juice of 1 lime (2–3 tablespoons), plus more to serve
1 tablespoon coconut flakes

8–10 round lettuce leaves

4 Assemble the wraps. Place a portion of the turnip rice in the middle of a lettuce leaf and top with a prawn. Repeat with remaining leaves, turnip rice, and prawns. Serve immediately, with additional lime juice squeezed over, if desired.

Try trimmed turnip noodles instead of turnip rice for a different texture.

Jalapeño Turkey Burgers with Coriander-Lime Kohlrabi Slaw

GF

P

MAKES
4 burgers

TIME TO PREPARE
20 minutes

TIME TO COOK
15 minutes

NUTRITIONAL INFORMATION
SERVING SIZE: **1 burger
and ¼ of kohlrabi slaw**
Calories: 347
Fat: 16g
Carbohydrates: 18g
Salt: 0.1g
Protein: 27g
Sugar: 8g

Ordering a burger at a restaurant and asking to replace the bun with a side salad is an easy trick for enjoying a burger without feeling stuffed. The only problem is that the usual side salad doesn't do justice to the burger. In this version, coriander, lime, jalapeño, and avocado go together even better than fish and chips making this burger with salad a winning combo. The subtle touch of jalapeño in the lean turkey burgers marries well with the tangy lime zest in the crunchy kohlrabi salad. Will you ever need burger buns again? Maybe not.

For the slaw

2 celery sticks, chopped

2 medium kohlrabi, peeled, spiralized with BLADE C

4 tablespoons lime juice

Grated zest of 1 lime

5g fresh coriander, chopped

1 tablespoon extra-virgin olive oil

1 tablespoon red wine vinegar

1 tablespoon honey

Salt and pepper

2 tablespoons fresh orange juice

For the burgers

2 small garlic cloves, finely chopped

Salt and pepper

450g lean turkey mince

2 teaspoons finely chopped jalapeño pepper

1 teaspoon ground coriander

2 tablespoons chopped fresh parsley

1 firm ripe avocado, diced

1 tablespoon extra-virgin olive oil

2 x 6mm-thick slices of beefsteak tomato

1 tablespoon fresh lime juice

1 Make the slaw. Combine the ingredients in a medium bowl. Place in the fridge to marinate while you prepare the burgers.

2 Make the burgers. Combine the garlic, salt and pepper, turkey, jalapeño, coriander, parsley, and avocado in a medium bowl. Using your hands, form two equal patties. Heat the olive oil in a large frying pan over a medium heat. When the oil is shimmering, add the burgers and cook for 3 minutes or until the bottoms are browned. Flip over and cook for another 3–5 minutes or until the burgers are cooked through. Transfer to a serving plate.

3 Using the same frying pan, over a medium-high heat, add the tomato slices and season with salt and pepper and the lime juice. Cook for 1 minute, flip over, and sear another 30 seconds on the other side, until the tomatoes are warmed through.

4 Top each burger with a tomato slice and serve with the kohlrabi slaw alongside.

It's important that the avocado is not overripe – slightly firm is best for stuffing into burgers. If it's too soft, it will make the whole burger mushy.

Rocket, Olive, and Onion Sweet Potato Pizza Stacks

MAKES
6 mini-pizzas

GF

Vt

TIME TO PREPARE
30 minutes

TIME TO COOK
30 minutes

NUTRITIONAL INFORMATION
SERVING SIZE: 1 mini-pizza
Calories: 273
Fat: 20g
Carbohydrates: 14g
Salt: 1.2g
Protein: 14g
Sugar: 6g

ALSO WORKS WELL WITH
Swedes • Potatoes •
Parsnips

It's definitely possible to cook spiralized vegetables together in a frying pan so that they form a pizza-like base, but it's tough to serve – the noodles tend to fall apart and the "crust" quickly becomes soggy. After a lot of experimenting, I found it easier to make mini-pizzas with a bun bottom, with each mini-pizza serving as a slice. These are great for parties, and the recipe can easily be doubled to serve twelve.

1 Preheat the oven to 230°C/450°F. Place a large non-stick frying pan over a medium heat and coat with cooking spray. When a little water flicked onto the frying pan sizzles, add the sweet potato noodles and season with garlic powder, salt, and pepper. Cover and cook for 5–7 minutes or until the noodles are softened and lightly browned.

2 Transfer the sweet potato noodles to a medium bowl, allow to cool for 1–2 minutes, then add the eggs and stir well. Fill six 10 x 4.5cm ramekins halfway with the noodles. Cover each with a piece of aluminium foil and push the foil down so that it's touching the noodles. Place a tin over the foil and press firmly to compress the noodles. Refrigerate for at least 15 minutes so that the noodles set.

Cooking spray

2 medium sweet potatoes, peeled, spiralized with **BLADE C**

1½ teaspoons garlic powder

Salt and pepper

2 medium eggs, lightly beaten

3½ tablespoons olive oil

½ red onion, thinly sliced

1 large garlic clove, finely chopped

Pinch of crushed dried chillies

6 tablespoons marinara sauce

1 (225g) ball or log of mozzarella cheese, thinly sliced

100g pitted green olives, halved

2 tablespoons grated Parmesan cheese

40g baby rocket

(recipe continues)

3 Heat ½ tablespoon olive oil in a medium non-stick frying pan over a medium-high heat. When the oil is shimmering, add the onion, garlic, and crushed dried chillies. Cook for 3–4 minutes or until the onion is wilted.

4 Heat 1 tablespoon olive oil in a large non-stick frying pan over a medium heat. When the oil is shimmering, add two of the buns, flipping the ramekins over the frying pan and patting the ramekin bottoms until the buns fall out. Cook for 3 minutes or until the noodles set, being sure to push in any stray noodles. Carefully flip and cook, flattening with the back of the spatula, another 2–3 minutes or until the bun is set and browned. Repeat with the remaining buns, adding 1 tablespoon oil for each batch.

5 Line a baking sheet with aluminium foil and coat the foil with cooking spray. Arrange the sweet potato buns in a single layer and top each bun with 1 tablespoon marinara sauce and some sliced mozzarella. Season with salt and pepper and bake for 5 minutes or until the cheese melts.

6 Remove the pizzas from the oven and cover evenly with the sautéed onion, the olives, and Parmesan cheese. Top with the rocket. Bring the buns together in a round to form a 'pizza', or serve individually.

You'll need six 10 x 4.5cm ramekins to make these mini-pizzas.

Apple-Potato Cheese Bun

MAKES
4 buns

GF

VT

TIME TO PREPARE
20 minutes

TIME TO COOK
15 minutes

NUTRITIONAL INFORMATION
SERVING SIZE: 1 bun
Calories: 171
Fat: 8g
Carbohydrates: 21g
Salt: 0.1g
Protein: 5g
Sugar: 4g

ALSO WORKS WELL WITH
Sweet Potatoes •
Parsnips

One of my oldest friends used to wow us with her ability to cook grilled cheese sandwiches perfectly in a frying pan when we were growing up. Not many kids knew how to cook – but Dana did. We'd go to her house to paint our nails and talk about boys. Afterwards, we'd watch her stand confidently over the hob, making grilled cheese. This Inspiralized adaptation is great for kids or for adults who want a healthier, gluten-free version of the classic sandwich.

1 Place a large non-stick frying pan over a medium heat and coat with cooking spray. Add the potato noodles and cover, cooking for 6–8 minutes, uncovering occasionally to toss, until the potato noodles start to brown, soften, and are cooked through.

2 In a large bowl, place the eggs, apple, potato noodles, and cheese. Toss to combine thoroughly and season with salt and pepper.

3 Place a small frying pan over a medium heat and add half of the olive oil. Once the oil shimmers, it's ready. Add one-quarter of the apple-potato mixture and place in the centre of the frying pan. Cook for 2–3 minutes or until the bottom of the bun is fully set. Flip over carefully, press down with a spatula to compact it, and cook for another 3–5 minutes or until the sandwich is completely firm.

4 Repeat with the remaining mixture and the rest of the olive oil, making 4 buns. Serve immediately.

Cooking spray

1 large potato, peeled, spiralized with **BLADE C**

2 eggs, beaten

1 apple, spiralized with **BLADE C**

45g Cheddar cheese, coarsely grated

Salt and pepper

1½ tablespoons extra-virgin olive oil

You can easily make this recipe into a bake for serving many by spreading out the potato and apple noodles in a baking dish, mixing them together with cheese, and then sprinkling some additional cheese on top before baking.

BAKES & GRATINS

Mediterranean Beetroot and Feta Frying Pan Bake

MAKES
4–6 servings

GF

TIME TO PREPARE
20 minutes

VT

TIME TO COOK
25 minutes

NUTRITIONAL INFORMATION
SERVING SIZE: ¹/₄ recipe
Calories: 148
Fat: 11g
Carbohydrates: 8g
Salt: 1.1g
Protein: 6g
Sugar: 5g

When Lu and I went on our first vacation together to Greece, everywhere we stopped we ordered a Greek salad and a regional beer. We quickly learned that the American version of this vegetarian salad was different from the real thing, which is lettuce-free and has predominantly thick-cut tomatoes with large chunks of feta. Here, I use the traditional salad mix for a hot dish. The combination of olives, onions, and fresh tomatoes is heavenly – the beetroot noodles only enhance all that flavour!

1 Preheat the oven to 200°C/400°F. In a large bowl, combine all the ingredients except the cheese and the parsley for garnish.

2 Place the block of feta or halloumi in the centre of a large ovenproof frying pan. Top and surround it with the beetroot noodle mixture. Cover with aluminium foil and bake for 20 minutes or until the beetroot noodles wilt. Serve hot, garnished with the remaining parsley.

Serve this with pitta chips and celery sticks as a starter, or enjoy it as a heartier main course topped with chickpeas, grilled prawns, or chicken.

85g yellow cherry tomatoes, halved

85g red cherry tomatoes, halved

2 medium garlic cloves, finely chopped

2 tablespoons chopped fresh parsley, plus 1 teaspoon for garnish

1 teaspoon dried oregano

1 tablespoon red wine vinegar

60g pitted Kalamata olives

1 tablespoon extra-virgin olive oil

2 small beetroots, peeled, spiralized with BLADE C

½ small red onion, peeled, spiralized with BLADE C

Salt and pepper

1 (225g) block of feta or halloumi cheese

Deconstructed Courgette Manicotti

MAKES
2 servings

GF

VT

TIME TO PREPARE
10 minutes

TIME TO COOK
40 minutes

NUTRITIONAL INFORMATION
SERVING SIZE: ½ **recipe**
Calories: 577
Fat: 26g
Carbohydrates: 63g
Salt: 3.1g
Protein: 33g
Sugar: 6g

When I make dinner, I'm usually cooking for one or two, but that's not to say I don't love a beef lasagne or a cheesy baked ziti – my favourite baked macaroni dish. This manicotti frying pan version was born of necessity: I was desperately craving manicotti – the Italian–American version of ricotta and spinach cannelloni – but I didn't want to buy all of the ingredients and have a ton of leftovers. So I made a frying pan version just for Lu and me: two mounds of manicotti filling nestled in courgette noodles, easy for sharing. The courgette noodles make the dish much lighter, fresher, and, frankly, more fun to eat. Without the starchy pasta you appreciate the decadent filling more, which is where most of the flavour is anyway.

1 Preheat the oven to 190°C/375°F.

2 Place a large cast-iron or non-stick frying pan over a medium heat and add the olive oil. When the oil is shimmering, add the garlic, crushed dried chillies, and onion, and cook for 2–3 minutes or until the onion is translucent. Add the tomatoes and their juices, season with salt and pepper, and stir. Increase the heat to medium-high and bring to the boil, then lower to a simmer. After 5 minutes, add the basil. Continue to simmer the sauce for 5 minutes more or until it is thickened.

3 Make the filling. Combine the cheeses and egg in a large bowl. Season with salt and pepper.

For the sauce

½ tablespoon olive oil

1 large garlic clove, finely chopped

Pinch of crushed dried chillies

60g red onion, chopped

400g tinned chopped tomatoes, no salt added

Salt and pepper

5 basil leaves, chopped

For the filling

20g Parmesan cheese, grated

200g ricotta cheese

2 tablespoons shredded mozzarella cheese, for topping

30g mozzarella cheese, shredded

1 small egg

Salt and pepper

Cooking spray

170g baby spinach

2 courgettes, spiralized with **BLADE A**

(recipe continues)

4 Place a medium non-stick ovenproof frying pan over a medium heat and coat with cooking spray. When some water flicked onto the frying pan sizzles, add the spinach and toss until wilted, about 2 minutes. Remove from the heat and fold into the cheese mixture.

5 Assemble the manicotti. Reserve half the sauce and spread the remaining sauce evenly on the bottom of the frying pan. Place the courgette noodles on top, then add the remaining sauce. Create two wells in the noodles and add the cheese filling. Sprinkle the mozzarella over the frying pan and season with pepper. Cover with aluminium foil and bake for 20–25 minutes or until the noodles have softened and the cheese is melted. Serve hot.

If you want to make this frying-pan dish into a bigger bake, double or triple the recipe to make either four or six pockets for the filling.

Vegetarian Carrot Enchilada Bake

MAKES
4–6 servings

GF
VT

TIME TO PREPARE
25 minutes

TIME TO COOK
35 minutes

NUTRITIONAL INFORMATION
SERVING SIZE: ¼ **recipe**
Calories: 360
Fat: 15g
Carbohydrates: 37g
Salt: 0.7g
Protein: 16g
Sugar: 7g

ALSO WORKS WELL WITH
Butternut Squash •
Swedes • Golden
Beetroot • Sweet
Potatoes

Basically, this recipe is a big vegetarian enchilada dish without the tortillas. Let's do the maths: subtracting the tortillas leaves us with the beans, sweetcorn, vegetables, and spices. Instead of preparing a flour-based enchilada sauce, we use tinned tomatoes and extra spices. *Plus* we have irresistible melted cheese on top. By removing the traditional starchy element, it's a much lighter yet still filling version of enchiladas.

Cooking spray

2 ears of sweetcorn, shucked and silks removed

1 tablespoon olive oil

1 teaspoon finely chopped garlic

85g white onion, diced

110g red pepper, diced

400g tinned black beans, drained and rinsed

1 jalapeño pepper, finely chopped

2 teaspoons ground cumin

2 teaspoons dried oregano

1 tablespoon chilli powder

2 tablespoons chopped fresh coriander

Salt and pepper

1 tablespoon fresh lime juice

400g tinned crushed tomatoes

3 large carrots, peeled, spiralized with **BLADE C**, then riced (see page 25)

90g mature Cheddar cheese, coarsely grated

45g pepper jack cheese, or any hard peppery cheese that will melt, grated

50g pitted black olives

(recipe continues)

1 Preheat the oven to 190°C/375°F. Coat a 4-litre baking dish with cooking spray.

2 Place the sweetcorn in a medium saucepan, cover with salted water, and bring to the boil over a high heat. Cook for 2 minutes or until the sweetcorn turns bright yellow and is easily pierced with a fork. Set aside to cool.

3 Heat the olive oil in a large pot over a medium heat. When the oil is shimmering, add the garlic, onion, and red pepper. Cook for 2–3 minutes or until the onion is translucent. Add the beans, jalapeño, cumin, oregano, chilli powder, and coriander. Slice the sweetcorn kernels into the pot with a knife, then season with salt, pepper, and lime juice. Toss to combine and cook for 2–3 minutes, until the flavours set. Add the tomatoes and carrot rice and cook for about 2 minutes to warm through. Transfer the mixture to the prepared baking dish.

4 Combine the cheeses in a small bowl, then sprinkle over the mixture in the dish. Cover with aluminium foil and bake for 15 minutes or until the carrot rice is cooked through. Uncover and bake for 5–10 minutes more or until the cheese is melted and begins to bubble. Serve warm, topped with the black olives.

This dish saves well for leftovers, so make a portion without the cheese and store it in the fridge in an airtight container. In the morning you can top it with a fried egg for a flavourful breakfast. Yum!

Swede Turkey Bake with Gruyère-Broccoli Breadcrumbs

MAKES
3–6 servings

GF

TIME TO PREPARE
20 minutes

TIME TO COOK
45 minutes

NUTRITIONAL INFORMATION
SERVING SIZE: ⅓ **recipe**
Calories: 34
Fat: 15g
Carbohydrates: 7g
Salt: 0.4g
Protein: 35g
Sugar: 4g

Swede noodles work well in bakes because they're resilient and they absorb flavours well. Swede is less starchy than other root vegetables, and when it roasts, it becomes sweet *and* savoury at once. The melted Gruyère adds elegant flavour and ensures that every bite is gooey and delectable. Top it all off with broccoli breadcrumbs to add a fluffy texture.

1 Preheat the oven to 200°C/400°F. Place a large saucepan over a medium heat and add the olive oil. When the oil is shimmering, add the garlic, crushed dried chillies, and onion. Cook for 2–3 minutes or until the onion is translucent. Push the mixture to the side of the frying pan and add the turkey to the centre. Season with oregano, salt, and pepper. Cook, breaking up the meat as it cooks, for 3–5 minutes or until browned. Stir to combine the ingredients in the pan.

2 Add the swede noodles and toss to combine. Cook for 5 minutes or until the noodles begin to soften. Transfer to a 4-litre baking dish.

3 Pulse the broccoli florets in a food processor until they take on a chunky, crumb-like consistency. In a medium bowl, combine the broccoli and the Gruyère, and season with salt and pepper. Evenly sprinkle the mixture over the casserole. Cover with aluminium foil and bake for 30 minutes or until the cheese is melted and the swede noodles are cooked through. Cut into portions and serve warm.

1 tablespoon olive oil

1 large garlic clove, finely chopped

Pinch of crushed dried chillies

½ white onion, thinly sliced

450g lean turkey mince

1 teaspoon dried oregano

Salt and pepper

1 medium swede, peeled, spiralized with
   BLADE C

60g broccoli florets

115g Gruyère cheese, grated

Waxy white potatoes offer a saltier flavour and can be easily substituted here for the swede.

Vegan Chipotle Carrot Macaroni Cheese

MAKES
4–6 servings

GF

V

TIME TO PREPARE
30 minutes

TIME TO COOK
25 minutes

NUTRITIONAL INFORMATION
SERVING SIZE: ¼ recipe
Calories: 267
Fat: 18g
Carbohydrates: 19g
Salt: 1.3g
Protein: 9g
Sugar: 6g

ALSO WORKS WELL WITH
Sweet Potatoes •
Beetroot • Butternut
Squash • Courgettes •
Swedes

This dish is the ultimate guilt-free macaroni cheese recipe: pastaless and cheeseless! How does that work, you ask? While the cashews provide thickness, the nutritional yeast adds that cheesy flavour. The natural sugar in the carrots is released as this dish bakes, making for an exquisite, sweet bite with a special chipotle kick. Don't ask any more questions – just make this recipe and enjoy it.

1 Preheat the oven to 180°C/350°F. Coat a 23 x 30cm baking dish with cooking spray.

2 Heat the olive oil in a non-stick frying pan over a medium-low heat. When the oil is shimmering, add the onion and garlic. Season with salt and pepper and cook for 2–3 minutes or until the onion is translucent. In a blender, combine the cooked onion and garlic, the cashews, stock, chillies, and nutritional yeast. Season with salt and pepper and continue to blend until creamy, about 1 minute.

3 Slice the carrots in half lengthways, then spiralize using blade B. Place the noodles in the baking dish and top with the cashew mixture. Cover with aluminium foil and bake for 20 minutes or until the carrot noodles are cooked through. Uncover and cook 5 minutes more or until lightly golden brown on top.

Cooking spray

1 tablespoon olive oil

60g white onion, chopped

3 medium garlic cloves, finely chopped

Salt and pepper

120g raw cashews

360ml reduced-salt vegetable stock

2 chipotle chillies in adobo sauce, finely chopped

2 tablespoons nutritional yeast flakes

2 large carrots, peeled

Don't have time for a baked dish? Simply cook the carrot noodles in a saucepan or boil in water for 2 minutes, then add the heated sauce for a quicker meal.

Parsnip and Kale Gratin

MAKES
4–6 servings

GF

VT

TIME TO PREPARE
20 minutes

TIME TO COOK
1 hour 20 minutes

NUTRITIONAL INFORMATION
SERVING SIZE: ¼ **recipe**
Calories: 391
Fat: 20g
Carbohydrates: 36g
Salt: 1.1g
Protein: 19g
Sugar: 5g

ALSO WORKS WELL WITH
Potatoes • Sweet
Potatoes • Swedes •
Beetroot • Butternut
Squash

If truth be told, I never understood the purpose of a gratin until I made my own, using parsnips instead of potatoes. Since parsnips are slightly sweet and nutty, they taste amazing with melted Gouda on top. Kale and garlic add texture while infusing the dish with nutrients. Although the parsnips look like potatoes in this gratin, they add extra nutrients and they lower the overall carbohydrate and calorie count. If you're looking for something to make or bring for a winter dinner or holiday party, try this gratin – the parsnips can be our little secret!

1 Preheat the oven to 220°C/425°F. Coat a 15 x 23cm baking dish with cooking spray. Slice the parsnips in half lengthways, being careful not to cut further down than the centre. Spiralize using blade A.

2 Heat the olive oil in a large frying pan over a medium heat. When the oil is shimmering, add the garlic and crushed dried chillies, and cook for 30 seconds or until fragrant. Add the kale and 2 teaspoons of the thyme, and season with salt and pepper. Sauté for 3–5 minutes or until the kale is cooked through and wilted.

3 Layer one-quarter of the parsnip noodles into the baking dish and top with one-third of the kale. Top with another quarter of the parsnip noodles, then a third of the Gouda, and season with ¼ teaspoon thyme. Add another layer of kale, a layer of parsnip noodles, another third of Gouda, and the remaining ¼ teaspoon thyme. Repeat once more, ending with the Gouda. Cover with aluminium foil and bake for 25–30 minutes or until the noodles are *al dente*.

Cooking spray

4 large parsnips, peeled

1 tablespoon olive oil

2 medium garlic cloves, finely chopped

¼ teaspoon crushed dried chillies

200g chopped fresh kale leaves

2½ teaspoons fresh thyme leaves

Salt and pepper

350g Gouda cheese, grated

Stuffed Vine Leaves Bake

MAKES
4–6 servings

GF

TIME TO PREPARE
30 minutes

V

TIME TO COOK
35 minutes

P

NUTRITIONAL INFORMATION
SERVING SIZE: ¼ **recipe**
Calories: 161
Carbohydrates: 17g
Salt: 0.6g
Protein: 3g
Sugar: 10g

ALSO WORKS WELL WITH
Golden Beetroot •
Swedes • Turnips

After a few failed attempts at stuffing vine leaves at home, I almost gave up – but I then decided to try them as a bake. As it turns out, the vine leaves work better this way: you get even more stuffing in every bite. Serve slices of this alongside a fresh salad with halloumi cheese and Kalamata olives, and you'll be transported straight to the Mediterranean.

1 Preheat the oven to 180°C/350°F. Coat a 2-litre baking dish with cooking spray.

2 Fill a medium saucepan with water and bring to the boil over a high heat. When the water is boiling, add the vine leaves. Cook for 1 minute to blanch, then drain and pat dry.

3 Heat 1 tablespoon olive oil in a large non-stick frying pan over a medium heat. When the oil is shimmering, add the garlic and cook for 30 seconds or until fragrant. Add the celeriac rice and toss, then add the stock and tomato. Generously season with salt and pepper and cook for 3–5 minutes, stirring occasionally, until the liquid has evaporated.

4 Transfer the mixture to a large bowl. Add the lemon juice, herbs, dried currants, and pine nuts. Stir to combine.

Cooking spray

225g jar brined vine leaves (or 25–30 fresh leaves)

2 tablespoons olive oil

4 medium garlic cloves, finely chopped

2 celeriac knobs, peeled, spiralized with BLADE C, then riced (see page 25)

360ml vegetable stock

85g deseeded and chopped ripe tomato

Salt and pepper

120ml fresh lemon juice

4 tablespoons chopped fresh dill

5 tablespoons chopped fresh parsley

3 tablespoons chopped fresh mint

65g currants or raisins

65g pine nuts

5 Line the bottom and sides of the baking dish with the vine leaves, overlapping and allowing them to hang over the sides. Spread the rice mixture in an even layer over the vine leaves. Top with another layer of vine leaves. Fold the overhanging vine leaves together, rolling them down into the dish and pinching tightly together to secure. Brush the top with the remaining 1 tablespoon olive oil and bake for 25–30 minutes or until the tops of the leaves darken and the mixture is firm.

Fennel Sausage and Butternut Squash Casserole

MAKES
4–6 servings

GF

TIME TO PREPARE
20 minutes

TIME TO COOK
40 minutes

NUTRITIONAL INFORMATION
SERVING SIZE: $^1/_4$ recipe
Calories: 573
Fat: 37g
Carbohydrates: 43g
Salt: 2.4g
Protein: 21g
Sugar: 13g

ALSO WORKS WELL WITH
Sweet Potatoes •
Swedes • Celeriac

When you combine seasonal ingredients at their peak, you get one super-flavourful dish. Case in point: this dish unites winter fennel with winter squash. The anise taste and the squash sweetness are truly symbiotic. And to top it all off, there's the rich, salty pecorino romano cheese. Escape the cold and enjoy the winter with this warm, inviting dish.

1 Preheat the oven to 190°C/375°F. Coat a 23 x 33cm baking dish with cooking spray.

2 Heat the olive oil in a large saucepan over a medium heat. When the oil is shimmering, add the sausage meat and onion. Cook for 5 minutes or until the sausage is browned. Add the crushed dried chillies and garlic, and cook for 30 seconds or until the garlic is fragrant. Then add the tomatoes, cheese, walnuts, and parsley. Stir in the butternut squash rice. Season with salt and pepper, and toss to combine.

3 Transfer the mixture to the prepared baking dish and spread evenly. Bake for 25–30 minutes or until the squash rice is softened and cooked through. Serve immediately.

Cooking spray

1 tablespoon olive oil

5 pork sausages with fennel, casings removed and meat crumbled

1 medium red onion, diced

½ teaspoon crushed dried chillies

3 medium garlic cloves, finely chopped

400g tinned chopped tomatoes, with juice

40g pecorino romano cheese, grated

120g walnuts, roughly chopped

3 tablespoons finely chopped fresh parsley

1 large butternut squash, peeled, spiralized with BLADE C, then riced (see page 25)

Salt and pepper

Chicken and Broccoli Frying Pan Bake

MAKES
4–6 servings

GF

TIME TO PREPARE
20 minutes

TIME TO COOK
40 minutes

NUTRITIONAL INFORMATION
SERVING SIZE: ¼ **recipe**
Calories: 428
Fat: 25g
Carbohydrates: 6g
Salt: 0.9g
Protein: 45g
Sugar: 2g

This chicken and broccoli bake is the best of both worlds. By replacing the traditional pasta with broccoli, you still have the *al dente* consistency of pasta but gain more nutrients and flavour. If your broccoli stems yield more half-moons than noodles, don't fret. The melted Havarti and Cheddar will pull everything together.

1 Preheat the oven to 200°C/400°F. Place a 30cm ovenproof frying pan over a medium heat and add 1 tablespoon olive oil. When the oil is shimmering, add the chicken, season with salt and pepper, and cook for 3 minutes per side or until lightly browned. Transfer to a plate along with any juices.

2 Bring a medium saucepan of salted water to the boil. Add the broccoli florets and noodles and cook until the florets are tender, 2–3 minutes. Drain.

3 Using the same frying pan, heat the remaining 2 tablespoons olive oil over a medium-high heat. When the oil is shimmering, add the garlic and onion, and cook for 2–3 minutes or until the onion is translucent. Whisk in the chicken stock and stir until the mixture thickens, about 2 minutes. Season with the thyme, parsley, and onion powder. Add the cooked chicken and the broccoli noodles and florets, and toss to combine. Top evenly with the cheeses.

4 Cover with aluminium foil and bake for 25 minutes or until bubbling. Remove the foil and grill for another 3–5 minutes or until the top turns golden brown.

3 tablespoons extra-virgin olive oil

450g boneless chicken breast, diced

Salt and pepper

2 large broccoli heads, florets removed, stems spiralized with BLADE C OR BLADE D

2 medium garlic cloves, finely chopped

60g white onion, chopped

120ml reduced-salt chicken stock

¼ teaspoon dried thyme

¼ teaspoon dried parsley

¼ teaspoon onion powder

90g mature Cheddar cheese, grated

45g Havarti cheese, grated

To add even more flavour and texture to this dish, toss in a cupful of spiralized sweet potato rice before baking.

RICE DISHES

Beetroot Superfood Bowl

Short Ribs with Sweet Potato "Grits"

Mustard and Herb-Crusted Rack of Lamb with "Couscous"

Teriyaki Salmon Balls with Ginger-Pineapple Rice

Pork Bibimbap with Ginger Gochugaru

Sweet Potato Fried Rice

Spicy Seafood-Chorizo Paella

Turnip-Stuffed Peppers with Parmesan

Vegetarian Chana Masala with Kohlrabi

Beetroot Superfood Bowl

MAKES
3–4 servings

TIME TO PREPARE
15 minutes

TIME TO COOK
15 minutes

NUTRITIONAL INFORMATION
SERVING SIZE: ¼ **recipe**
Calories: 312
Fat: 14g
Carbohydrates: 38g
Salt: 0.4g
Protein: 12g
Sugar: 14g

You've probably heard the word *superfood* used a million times before, but what does it actually mean? Superfoods are low in calories and high in nutrients. What happens when you eat several superfoods in one dish? Your skin will glow, you'll rev up your metabolism, and you'll boost your immune system. I often make this dish when I need a burst of energy and nutrients before a gruelling travel schedule.

1 Rinse the quinoa and place in a small saucepan with the water. Bring to the boil over a high heat, then lower the heat and simmer for 15 minutes or until the quinoa is fluffy. If the quinoa is not yet fluffy, add 60ml water and continue to cook, repeating as necessary until fluffy.

2 In a large bowl, combine the beetroot rice, spinach, almonds, avocado, and edamame.

3 In a small bowl, whisk together the dressing ingredients.

4 Add the quinoa to the beetroot rice mixture, pour the dressing on top, and toss. Serve immediately.

85g uncooked quinoa

360ml water

2 medium beetroots, peeled, spiralized with BLADE C, then riced (see page 25)

120g fresh spinach

25g flaked almonds

1 avocado, cubed

120g cooked edamame beans

For the dressing

60ml apple cider vinegar

2 tablespoons fresh lime juice

1 tablespoon chopped fresh mint

2 tablespoons honey

Salt and pepper

Short Ribs with
Sweet Potato "Grits"

MAKES
2–3 servings

GF

TIME TO PREPARE
15 minutes

TIME TO COOK
2 hours 30 minutes

NUTRITIONAL INFORMATION
SERVING SIZE: ⅓ **recipe**
Calories: 527
Fat: 34g
Carbohydrates: 26g
Salt: 2.3g
Protein: 29g
Sugar: 10g

ALSO WORKS WELL WITH
Swedes • Carrots

I never thought about applying to universities in the South – until I tagged along on a road trip to North Carolina with my mum to drop off my sister at summer camp. Tired from all the driving, we snuggled into a local restaurant and asked the waitress to bring us "something Southern". What did we get? A big bowl of grits. I didn't like their bland taste and couldn't even get a full spoonful down, but a few years later, during my freshman year at Wake Forest University (also in North Carolina), I decided to give them a second try. I ordered prawns and grits for dinner, and they were wonderful because they were cheese grits! Whether you prefer your grits simple or with cheese, at breakfast, lunch, or dinner, you'll love this version, using sweet potato rice instead of hominy grits, paired with melt-in-your-mouth short ribs.

For the short ribs

450g boneless short ribs

Salt and pepper

1 tablespoon olive oil

115g white onion, chopped

2 medium sticks celery, chopped

2 medium garlic cloves, finely chopped

180ml hearty red wine (such as Chianti)

675g tinned chopped tomatoes

360ml reduced-salt beef stock

For the cheese "grits"

1 tablespoon olive oil

1 medium garlic clove, finely chopped

1 large sweet potato, peeled, spiralized with BLADE C, then riced (see page 25)

Salt and pepper

240ml reduced-salt beef stock

4 teaspoons finely chopped fresh parsley

45g mature Cheddar cheese, grated

1 Make the short ribs. Preheat the oven to 180°C/350°F. Season the short ribs generously with salt and pepper. Heat the olive oil in a large casserole dish or ovenproof pot over a medium-high heat. When the oil is shimmering, add the short ribs, being sure not to crowd the pan. Brown for 3–4 minutes per side, then transfer to a plate.

2 Reduce the heat to medium-low. Add the onion, celery, and garlic and cook for 2–3 minutes or until the onion is translucent. Add the wine, tomatoes, and stock, and season again with salt and pepper. Increase the heat to high and bring to the boil, then reduce to low and add the short ribs. Cover and transfer to the oven to cook for about 2½ hours or until the meat is very tender.

3 Make the cheese 'grits'. Heat 1 tablespoon olive oil in a large pot over a medium heat. When the oil is shimmering, add the garlic and cook for 30 seconds or until fragrant. Add the sweet potato rice, season with salt and pepper, and stir. Cook for 2 minutes to heat through, then add the stock. Turn the heat to low and simmer for 10–15 minutes or until the stock has evaporated. Stir in 3 teaspoons of the parsley, then remove the pot from the heat and fold in the cheese. Stir until the cheese has melted.

4 Spoon the sweet potato rice into bowls and top with the short ribs and a spoonful of juices from the pot. Sprinkle with the remaining 1 teaspoon parsley and serve hot.

For more of a sweetcorn taste, add 120g puréed cooked sweetcorn to the sweet potato rice mixture.

Mustard and Herb-Crusted Rack of Lamb with "Couscous"

MAKES
4 servings

TIME TO PREPARE
25 minutes

TIME TO COOK
30 minutes

NUTRITIONAL INFORMATION
SERVING SIZE: ¼ **recipe**
Calories: 437
Fat: 30g
Carbohydrates: 25g
Salt: 1.9g
Protein: 20g
Sugar: 12g

ALSO WORKS WELL WITH
Sweet Potatoes •
Carrots • Beetroot •
Kohlrabi

Cooking a rack of lamb can be intimidating, but this recipe is much easier than it looks. It could become your go-to meal for guests. The meat is well seasoned and the flavour and consistency of the turnip rice are unique, so it's sure to be a hit. The turnip rice fluffs up as it simmers in the vegetable stock, creating a couscous-like texture with the deep flavour suitable for accompanying such an impressive meat.

For the breadcrumbs

1 slice wholemeal bread, torn into pieces

1 medium garlic clove, chopped

1 tablespoon chopped fresh thyme leaves

1 tablespoon chopped fresh rosemary leaves

1 teaspoon chopped fresh parsley

For the lamb

1 rack of lamb (8 ribs)

Salt and pepper

1 tablespoon olive oil

1–1½ tablespoons wholegrain or country-style Dijon mustard

For the turnip rice

1 yellow pepper, stem removed

1 tablespoon olive oil

1 large garlic clove, finely chopped

1 medium red onion, thinly sliced

5 celery sticks, finely diced

4 large turnips, peeled, spiralized with BLADE C, then riced (see page 25)

Salt and pepper

180ml reduced-salt chicken stock

Chopped fresh parsley, for garnish

(recipe continues)

1 Preheat the oven to 200°C/400°F. Line a baking tray with parchment paper.

2 Prepare the breadcrumbs. Combine the ingredients in a food processor and pulse until crumb-like.

3 Roast the lamb. Season the rack with salt and pepper. Place a large griddle pan or cast-iron frying pan over a medium heat and add the olive oil. When the oil is shimmering, add the lamb, fat side down, and sear for 1–2 minutes. Flip over and cook for 1 more minute to lightly sear on the other side. Remove from the heat and spread the mustard over the fat side of the rack. Sprinkle the breadcrumbs over the mustard and gently press down to fully adhere. Transfer to the prepared baking tray and roast for 20–25 minutes or until cooked to your liking.

4 Make the turnip rice. Place the yellow pepper directly over the hob flame and char it all over, turning occasionally, until the skin is almost completely blackened, about 10 minutes. (If you do not have a gas hob, heat the grill and line a baking sheet with aluminum foil. Slice off the top of the pepper and remove the seeds. Slice the pepper in half and lay, skin side up, on the foil. Set the sheet 12–13cm away from the heat source and grill for 5–10 minutes or until peppers are blackened all over.) Transfer to an airtight container to cool.

5 Place a large non-stick frying pan over a medium heat and add the olive oil. When the oil is shimmering, add the garlic, onion, and celery; cook for 2–3 minutes or until the onion is translucent. Add the turnip rice and season with salt and pepper. Pour in the chicken stock and cook for 5–7 minutes or until the turnip rice begins to brown slightly.

6 Remove the pepper from the container and peel off the charred skin. Halve the pepper, then remove and discard the seeds. Slice lengthways into strips. Add the roasted pepper to the turnip rice.

7 Remove the lamb from the oven and allow it to rest on a chopping board for 5 minutes. Divide the turnip rice among four plates. Carve the rack of lamb into eight individual ribs and place two ribs on top of each plate of turnip rice. Garnish with parsley and serve.

Teriyaki Salmon Balls with Ginger-Pineapple Rice

MAKES
3 servings

TIME TO PREPARE
20 minutes

TIME TO COOK
20 minutes

NUTRITIONAL INFORMATION
SERVING SIZE: 1/3 recipe
Calories: 336
Fat: 13g
Carbohydrates: 28g
Salt: 2.4g
Protein: 28g
Sugar: 16g

ALSO WORKS WELL WITH
Sweet Potatoes •
Beetroot • Kohlrabi

These salmon balls happened accidentally. I was making dinner for Lu and me, but realized I had only one small salmon fillet. Since the rest of the recipe was already prepped, I started to make salmon burgers, but I had no breadcrumbs. Staring into my fridge, I spotted a few broccoli florets and had the idea to turn *them* into breadcrumbs. The result? Perfectly soft salmon balls with a subtle hint of warm broccoli! I'll never make them any other way again!

For the teriyaki sauce
60ml reduced-salt soy sauce

1 medium garlic clove, finely chopped

1 teaspoon grated fresh ginger

1 tablespoon honey

2 tablespoons mirin

Pepper

For the salmon balls
30g broccoli florets

280g salmon fillet, skin removed

2 tablespoons finely chopped shallots

2 teaspoons finely chopped garlic

Salt and pepper

For the rice
1 tablespoon virgin coconut oil

1 teaspoon finely chopped fresh ginger

1 teaspoon finely chopped garlic

35g spring onions, green and white parts, chopped

2 large carrots, peeled, spiralized with BLADE C, then riced (see page 25)

135g diced pineapple

Salt and pepper

(recipe continues)

1 Preheat the oven to 200°C/400°F. Line a baking tray with parchment paper.

2 Make the teriyaki sauce. Whisk the ingredients in a small bowl and set aside.

3 Make the salmon balls. Place the broccoli florets in a food processor and pulse until the consistency of breadcrumbs. Add the salmon, shallots, garlic, and salt and pepper. Pulse until the salmon breaks into small pieces and the broccoli crumbs are evenly dispersed. Using your hands, form the mixture into nine 2.5cm balls and place on the prepared baking tray. Bake for 11–13 minutes, flipping over halfway through.

4 Brush the salmon balls with some of the teriyaki sauce. Return the salmon balls to the oven and bake for 5 minutes more.

5 Prepare the rice. Place a large non-stick frying pan over a medium heat and add the coconut oil. When the oil is shimmering, add the ginger, garlic, and spring onions. Cook until fragrant, about 30 seconds, then add the carrot rice, pineapple chunks, and 1 tablespoon of the teriyaki sauce. Season with salt and pepper and toss to combine. Cook for 5–7 minutes or until slightly softened.

6 Divide the rice into portions and top each with three salmon balls.

These salmon balls pair well with courgette noodles sautéed with ginger, garlic, and sesame oil.

Pork Bibimbap with Ginger Gochugaru

MAKES
2 servings

TIME TO PREPARE
20 minutes

TIME TO COOK
15 minutes

NUTRITIONAL INFORMATION
SERVING SIZE: ½ recipe
Calories: 489
Fat: 28g
Carbohydrates: 23g
Salt: 1.1g
Protein: 38g
Sugar: 12g

ALSO WORKS WELL WITH
Courgettes • Carrots •
Turnips

Everything tastes better with a fried egg on top! Bibimbap is a Korean dish of rice and mixed vegetables. Before you dig in, though, you're supposed to stir the ingredients together to unify it. What makes it unified? The egg! When the yolk breaks, it coats the ingredients and marries for a complex bite loaded with flavour. But the daikon radish here becomes the star of this rice bowl once it's cooked with the ginger, garlic, spring onions, and *gochugaru*.

1½ tablespoons virgin coconut oil or vegetable oil

225g lean pork mince

2 teaspoons reduced-salt soy sauce

1½ tablespoons finely chopped garlic

Salt and pepper

1 teaspoon finely chopped fresh ginger

35g spring onions, green and white parts, diced

2 large daikon radishes, peeled, spiralized with BLADE C OR BLADE D, then riced (see page 25) and drained

½ teaspoon *gochugaru* or chilli powder

½ tablespoon toasted sesame oil

120g fresh spinach

Cooking spray

2 medium eggs

½ teaspoon white sesame seeds

1 medium cucumber, spiralized with BLADE C and patted dry

(recipe continues)

1 Place a large non-stick frying pan over a medium heat and add ½ tablespoon coconut oil. When the oil is shimmering, add the pork and cook, breaking it up with a wooden spoon. Add the soy sauce and 1 tablespoon garlic, and season with salt and pepper. Cook for about 5 minutes or until the pork is browned. Transfer to a bowl and cover.

2 In the same frying pan, over a medium heat, add the remaining 1 tablespoon coconut oil. When the oil is shimmering, add the ginger and remaining ½ teaspoon garlic and cook for 30 seconds or until fragrant. Stir in the spring onions and daikon rice. Cook for 1 minute or until the rice begins to turn light brown, then sprinkle on the gochugaru. Stir to combine and cook for about 5 minutes to heat the daikon rice through, stirring frequently. Transfer to a bowl and cover.

3 In the same frying pan, heat the sesame oil over a medium heat. When the oil is shimmering, add the spinach and cook until wilted, tossing frequently, about 2 minutes. Transfer to a plate.

4 Return the frying pan to a medium heat and coat with cooking spray. Crack in the eggs and cook without stirring for 3–5 minutes or until the egg whites are set and the yolks are still runny.

5 Evenly divide the daikon rice, pork, spinach, and cucumber noodles between two bowls. Sprinkle the sesame seeds over the spinach. Top each bowl with a fried egg and serve immediately.

A Korean chilli powder made from dried gochu chillies, *gochugaru* can be difficult to find in some supermarkets. If you don't have an Asian market near you, you can order it online. There's no proper substitute, and you'll love this dish so much that I promise you'll use the *gochugaru* again.

Sweet Potato Fried Rice

MAKES
225g rice

GF

TIME TO PREPARE
10 minutes

VT

TIME TO COOK
10 minutes

P

NUTRITIONAL INFORMATION
SERVING SIZE: $^1/_2$ **recipe**
Calories: 236
Carbohydrates: 22g
Salt: 0.6g
Protein: 10g
Sugar: 7g

ALSO WORKS WELL WITH
Carrots • Beetroot •
Kohlrabi • Turnips •
Daikon Radishes •
Butternut Squash

When I first started spiralizing, I tried to re-create all my favourite carb dishes, and fried rice was number one on my list. Introduce me to someone who doesn't love fried rice, because I'd love to meet that person. It's a takeaway classic! This Inspiralized version mimics the original and tastes even better when chilled as leftovers – just like the real deal!

1 Heat the oil in a large non-stick frying pan over a medium heat. When the oil is shimmering, add the onion and cook for 2 minutes or until translucent. Add the sweet potato rice and the stock, season with salt and pepper, and cook for 1 minute, stirring frequently to warm the rice. Reduce the heat and simmer, allowing the liquid to evaporate, about 5 minutes. If the rice is still crunchy, stir and cook for another 2 minutes.

2 Heat a medium non-stick frying pan over a medium heat. When a bit of water flicked onto the frying pan sizzles, add the eggs and briefly scramble them.

3 Fold the scrambled eggs and the peas into the sweet potato rice mixture. Add the soy sauce and toss to combine. Serve hot.

1 tablespoon vegetable, olive, or coconut oil

½ medium white onion, diced

1 large sweet potato, peeled, spiralized with **BLADE C**, then riced (see page 25)

120ml reduced-salt vegetable or chicken stock

Salt and pepper

2 medium eggs, lightly beaten

60g cooked frozen or fresh green peas

1 teaspoon reduced-salt soy sauce

For a stickier fried rice, omit the stock and double the oil. This way, the rice will take longer to soften and will brown along the way.

Spicy Seafood-Chorizo Paella

MAKES
4–5 servings

GF

TIME TO PREPARE
20 minutes

P

TIME TO COOK
25 minutes

NUTRITIONAL INFORMATION
SERVING SIZE: ¼ **recipe**
Calories: 158
Fat: 4g
Carbohydrates: 17g
Salt: 0.8g
Protein: 13g
Sugar: 7g

ALSO WORKS WELL WITH
Kohlrabi • Butternut
Squash • Beetroot

When I studied abroad, I dreamed about visiting Barcelona. I wasn't dreaming of gorgeous people in high fashion, the outstanding architecture, the striking scenery, or a rich history and culture. No, I was dreaming of paella – big frying pans of it filled with meats, seafood, and Spanish seasonings. Once there, every paella, whether a tapas portion or dinner size, left me awestruck. This paella is a healthier, simplified version of one of the world's truly memorable dishes.

1 Heat the olive oil in a large frying pan over a medium heat. When the oil is shimmering, add the garlic, crushed dried chillies, onion, and green pepper. Cook for 2–3 minutes or until vegetables soften. Add the chorizo and cook for 2–3 minutes or until it begins to brown. Add the tomatoes, peas, carrot rice, chilli powder, paprika, turmeric, lemon juice, coriander, salt, and pepper. Stir to combine.

2 Press the cod and prawns into the rice. Cover the frying pan and allow the mixture to cook undisturbed for 5–7 minutes or until the seafood is cooked through. Garnish with parsley and serve immediately.

If you have a paella pan, use it. If not, the largest, deepest frying pan you have will do just fine.

1 tablespoon olive oil

1 tablespoon finely chopped garlic

¼ teaspoon crushed dried chillies

55g yellow onion, diced

1 small green pepper, diced

1 large chorizo sausage, thinly sliced (about 6mm)

400g tinned chopped tomatoes

60g frozen peas

2 large carrots, peeled, spiralized with **BLADE C**, then riced (see page 25)

1 teaspoon chilli powder

1 teaspoon smoked paprika

½ teaspoon ground turmeric

2 tablespoons fresh lemon juice

1 tablespoon chopped fresh coriander

Salt and pepper

115g cod fillet, chopped into 2.5cm cubes

12 medium prawns, defrosted if frozen, peeled and deveined

2 teaspoons finely chopped fresh parsley

Turnip-Stuffed Peppers with Parmesan

MAKES
6–8 pepper halves

GF

VT

TIME TO PREPARE
15 minutes

TIME TO COOK
40 minutes

NUTRITIONAL INFORMATION
SERVING SIZE: 1 pepper half
Calories: 132
Fat: 10g
Carbohydrates: 3g
Salt: 0.4g
Protein: 7g
Sugar: 2g

ALSO WORKS WELL WITH
Celeriac • Butternut Squash • Sweet Potatoes

One of the first things I ever cooked for myself was quinoa-stuffed peppers, using a recipe from *Vegetarian Times*. That dish inspired this one. It seems super fancy, but it's easy to make. I love anything I can pop in the oven and serve without having to worry about plating – it looks gorgeous on its own. When you slice into these peppers, the coriander and lightly spiced turnip rice transport you to Mexico, but with an Italian twist added by the salty Parmesan cheese.

1 Preheat the oven to 190°C/375°F. Coat a rimmed baking tray or shallow baking dish with cooking spray.

2 Heat the olive oil in a large saucepan over a medium heat. When the oil is shimmering, add the garlic and onion. Cook for 2 minutes or until the onion is translucent.

3 Add the avocado, coriander, olives, turnip rice, oregano, cumin, and chilli powder. Season with salt and pepper and stir to combine. Cook for 2–3 minutes to allow the turnip rice to fully absorb the flavours and take on the colours of the seasonings.

4 Transfer the mixture to a large bowl, add half the cheese, and toss well.

Cooking spray

½ tablespoon olive oil

2 teaspoons finely chopped garlic

60g red onion, chopped

1 avocado, cubed

1 tablespoon chopped fresh coriander

55g pitted black olives, quartered

1 small turnip, peeled, spiralized with **BLADE C**, then riced (see page 25) and drained

½ teaspoon dried oregano

¼ teaspoon ground cumin

1 teaspoon chilli powder

Salt and pepper

75g Parmesan cheese, grated

4 large green peppers

(recipe continues)

5 Slice off and discard the tops of the peppers, halve them lengthways, and discard the seeds and any white flesh. Stuff the pepper halves with as much turnip rice mixture as possible, and place on the baking tray. Sprinkle the remaining Parmesan over the stuffed peppers.

6 Cover the peppers with aluminium foil and bake for 20 minutes. Remove the foil and continue baking for 5 minutes more or until the cheese is bubbling and beginning to brown on top. Serve hot.

Make the Spicy Sweet Potato Strings (page 56) and save some leftovers for this recipe. Throw them into a food processor, pulse until rice-like, and add them to the stuffing mixture. This trick will save you time *and* add more spice to the peppers.

Vegetarian Chana Masala with Kohlrabi

MAKES
4 servings

TIME TO PREPARE
15 minutes

TIME TO COOK
30 minutes

NUTRITIONAL INFORMATION
SERVING SIZE: 1/4 **recipe**
Calories: 457
Fat: 9g
Carbohydrates: 67g
Salt: 1.4g
Protein: 21g
Sugar: 13g

ALSO WORKS WELL WITH
Carrots • Celeriac •
Butternut Squash •
Beetroot • Sweet
Potatoes

The beauty of using spiralized vegetables is that they add freshness and lightness to even the heaviest of dishes, such as this south Indian chickpea curry. The flavours are deep, aromatic, and thick, while the kohlrabi is crisp and deliciously refreshing.

1 tablespoon virgin coconut oil

1 white onion, diced

3 large garlic cloves, finely chopped

1 tablespoon finely chopped fresh ginger

1 serrano chilli, deseeded and finely chopped

1½ teaspoon garam masala

1½ teaspoons ground coriander

2 teaspoons ground cumin

½ teaspoon ground turmeric

¼ teaspoon cayenne pepper

Salt

800g tinned chopped tomatoes

1 tablespoon fresh lemon juice

800g tinned chickpeas, drained and rinsed

2 large kohlrabi, peeled, spiralized with BLADE C, then riced (see page 25)

140g natural 0% fat Greek yogurt

1½ tablespoons chopped fresh coriander

(recipe continues)

1 In a large saucepan, heat the oil over a medium heat. When the oil is shimmering, add the onion, garlic, ginger, and chilli. Cook for about 3 minutes or until the onion turns translucent. Add the garam masala, coriander, cumin, turmeric, and cayenne pepper. Season with salt and cook for 2 more minutes or until the vegetables absorb the spices. Add the tomatoes and lemon juice, increase the heat to high, bring to the boil, and add the chickpeas. Then reduce the heat to low and simmer for 10–15 minutes to let the flavours develop.

2 Place a large non-stick frying pan over a medium heat. When a little water flicked onto the frying pan sizzles, add the kohlrabi rice. Cook for 3–5 minutes, stirring frequently or until softened and warmed through. Remove the pan from the heat and set aside.

3 Stir the yogurt and coriander into the chickpeas. Serve in bowls alongside the kohlrabi rice.

To make use of the thick kohlrabi greens, chop them up and add about 225g to the simmering curry.

PASTAS & NOODLES

Beetroot Pasta with Blood Orange, Honey Walnuts, and Crispy Kale

Sesame Almond Butter Kohlrabi Bowl

Bacon Cacio e Pepe

Pesto Spaghetti with Heirloom Cherry Tomatoes

Spicy Garlic Crab with Parsnips

Courgette Linguine with Garlic Clam Sauce

Halibut en Papillote with Butternut Squash

Bikini Bolognese

Albondigas and Courgettes with Tomato-Serrano Sauce

Thai Drunken Courgette Noodles with Pork

Vegan Celeriac Alfredo with Tenderstem Broccoli

Sweet Potato Carbonara

Seared Tuna with Chimichurri

Pesto Turnips with Shredded Brussels Sprouts

Tofu Miso-Tahini Carrot Bowl

Beetroot Pasta with Blood Orange, Honey Walnuts, and Crispy Kale

MAKES
2 servings

TIME TO PREPARE
15 minutes

TIME TO COOK
20 minutes

NUTRITIONAL INFORMATION
SERVING SIZE: ½ **recipe**
Calories: 383
Fat: 26g
Carbohydrates: 33g
Salt: 0.4g
Protein: 7g
Sugar: 15g

ALSO WORKS WELL WITH
Golden Beetroot •
Butternut Squash

When you're a food blogger, you are especially aware of produce seasonality. You know it's autumn when your Twitter feed is full of pumpkin everything – lattes, cookies, pancakes, smoothies, granola, you name it. One day, I signed on to learn that blood oranges were in season and I had almost missed out on them! I rushed to the supermarket, picked up a few, and headed back to the kitchen to make a recipe before my small window of relevancy closed. I was happy I did – when you roast an orange, it somehow transforms into a velvety, luxurious, and sweetened version of itself.

For the vinaigrette
Juice from ¼ large lemon

Salt and pepper

1 tablespoon olive oil

1 tablespoon water

2 teaspoons red wine vinegar

60ml fresh orange juice

1 teaspoon wholegrain or country-style Dijon mustard

For the salad
2 medium beetroots, peeled, spiralized with BLADE C

Olive oil

Salt and pepper

Cooking spray

1 large blood orange, peeled and quartered or cut into eighths

75g roughly chopped kale leaves (stems removed)

50g walnuts

Raw honey

You can always buy kale crisps instead of roasting your own, but if you have the time, make them fresh and save the leftovers for snacking.

(recipe continues)

1 Make the vinaigrette. Whisk the ingredients in a small bowl and refrigerate.

2 Prepare the salad. Preheat the oven to 190°C/375°F. Place the beetroot noodles on a baking tray and drizzle lightly with olive oil. Season with salt and pepper and roast in the oven for 15 minutes.

3 Lightly coat a separate baking tray with cooking spray and place the orange pieces on one side and the kale on the other. Lightly coat the kale with the cooking spray and season with salt and pepper. Bake for 10–12 minutes, then transfer the kale to a platter.

4 Add the walnuts where the kale was. Drizzle lightly with honey and toss carefully with tongs. Return the baking tray to the oven for 5 minutes more or until the nuts are lightly toasted.

5 Divide the roasted beetroot noodles among serving plates and top with the orange pieces, walnuts, and kale. Drizzle the vinaigrette over and serve.

Sesame Almond Butter Kohlrabi Bowl

MAKES
3 servings

TIME TO PREPARE
15 minutes

TIME TO COOK
15 minutes

NUTRITIONAL INFORMATION
SERVING SIZE: $^1/_3$ **recipe**
Calories: 410
Fat: 31g
Carbohydrates: 23g
Salt: 1.5g
Protein: 15g
Sugar: 11g

ALSO WORKS WELL WITH
Courgettes •
Cucumbers

This dish is a spin on peanut noodles. Almond butter is higher in micronutrients, such as calcium, iron, magnesium, and vitamin E. The real star, though, is the kohlrabi noodles, which refresh every bite with their light taste and crunchy skin. The longer the kohlrabi sits in the dressing, the more infused it will become with flavour, so pop this dish in the fridge and enjoy it later.

1 Combine the almond butter, soy sauce, honey, sesame oil, lime juice, water, and salt and pepper in a food processor and pulse until creamy. Transfer to a bowl.

2 Rinse the food processor and wipe dry. Add the almonds and pulse until chunky ground, taking care not to grind into a powder.

3 Place the kohlrabi noodles in a medium bowl with the spring onions. Add the almond butter sauce and the ground almonds, and toss to combine thoroughly. Top with the sesame seeds. Chill in the fridge or serve immediately.

115g smooth almond butter

3 tablespoons reduced-salt soy sauce

1 tablespoon honey

1 teaspoon toasted sesame oil

1 tablespoon fresh lime juice

1 tablespoon water

Salt and pepper

20g flaked almonds

2 kohlrabi, spiralized with BLADE B

45g spring onions, green and white parts, chopped

2 teaspoons white sesame seeds

Bacon Cacio e Pepe

MAKES
2 servings

TIME TO PREPARE
10 minutes

TIME TO COOK
15 minutes

NUTRITIONAL INFORMATION
SERVING SIZE: ½ **recipe**
Calories: 161
Fat: 9g
Carbohydrates: 6g
Salt: 0.9g
Protein: 9g
Sugar: 3g

ALSO WORKS WELL WITH
Parsnips • Broccoli
• Butternut Squash •
Kohlrabi

Simple, sexy, and decadent, this dish has the cheeses melting together perfectly with the warmed courgette noodles and meshing with the bacon and pepper for a taste so creamy and light you'll find it hard to believe you're not eating pasta. Most importantly, you can enjoy your romantic evening without feeling bloated. Ladies, if you have a hard time convincing your man to eat courgette noodles, make him this dish – he'll be a believer after that first bite!

1 Heat a large frying pan over a medium heat and coat lightly with cooking spray. When a bit of water flicked onto the frying pan sizzles, add the bacon and cook until crisp. Drain the bacon on a kitchen paper-lined plate.

2 Add the garlic and crushed dried chillies to the frying pan, still over a medium heat, and cook for 30 seconds or until fragrant. Add the courgette noodles and cook, tossing, for 2–3 minutes or until the noodles are *al dente*. Generously season with pepper and add the cheeses, tossing to combine thoroughly until the noodles are coated with cheese.

3 Divide between two bowls, topping each serving with more pepper and Parmesan cheese, as desired. Crumble the bacon on top and serve.

Cooking spray

3 rashers streaky bacon

1 large garlic clove, finely chopped

Pinch of crushed dried chillies

2 medium courgettes, spiralized with
   BLADE C

Cracked black peppercorns

4 tablespoons grated pecorino romano cheese

4 tablespoons grated Parmesan cheese, plus more for garnish

To make your courgette noodles look more like pasta noodles, peel off the vegetable's green skin before you spiralize, as in this picture.

Pesto Spaghetti with Heirloom Cherry Tomatoes

MAKES
3 servings

VT

GF

TIME TO PREPARE
20 minutes

NUTRITIONAL INFORMATION
SERVING SIZE: 1/3 **recipe**
Calories: 277
Fats: 26g
Carbohydrates: 8g
Salt: 0.3g
Protein: 6g
Sugar: 4g

ALSO WORKS WELL WITH
Beetroot • Kohlrabi

Next to a simple *pomodoro*, pesto is the quintessential pasta sauce. Its classic Italian taste can bring any pasta to life. Here, paired with courgette noodles, it showcases the power of vegetable pasta. You're suddenly at a trattoria in Italy yet maintaining that slim waistline! If you have hesitated to start with the spiralizer, I recommend trying this recipe – it's simple, quick to make, and will absolutely please your taste buds.

1 Combine the basil, pine nuts, olive oil, salt and pepper, garlic, and Parmesan in a food processor and pulse until creamy.

2 Place the courgette noodles and tomatoes in a large bowl, pour the pesto on top, and toss to combine. Serve.

100g fresh basil leaves

3 tablespoons pine nuts

60ml olive oil

½ teaspoon freshly ground sea salt

¼ teaspoon freshly ground black pepper

1 large garlic clove, finely chopped

3 tablespoons grated Parmesan cheese

2 medium courgettes, spiralized with **BLADE C**

125g mixed heirloom cherry tomatoes

If you prefer this dish hot, heat the courgette noodles in a large frying pan over a medium heat for 2–3 minutes. When they are *al dente*, add the tomatoes and pesto, and toss for another 1–2 minutes or until heated through.

Spicy Garlic Crab with Parsnips

MAKES
2 servings

GF
P

TIME TO PREPARE
15 minutes

TIME TO COOK
15 minutes

NUTRITIONAL INFORMATION
SERVING SIZE: ½ **recipe**
Calories: 312
Fat: 14g
Carbohydrates: 27g
Salt: 1g
Protein: 22g
Sugar: 7g

ALSO WORKS WELL WITH
Courgettes •
Daikon Radishes •
Kohlrabi

While all the recipes in this cookbook are irresistibly delicious, I really mean it about this one. Parsnips are one of those vegetables that sometimes invoke a "meh" or "blah" feeling; they're usually just mashed or roasted in a medley with other root vegetables. When I started spiralizing them, though, I learned to love parsnips in a whole new way. In this dish, their sweetness works fabulously with the crab, which is prized for its own delicate, sweet taste. Now, see if you also won't be able to put your fork down.

1 Heat the olive oil in a large frying pan over a medium heat. When the oil is shimmering, add the garlic and crushed dried chillies and cook for 30 seconds or until fragrant.

2 Add the parsnip noodles and season generously with salt and pepper. Cover and cook for 1–3 minutes or until the parsnip noodles are softened but still *al dente*, uncovering and tossing occasionally.

3 Add the crab and lemon juice, and cook for 2 minutes more or until the parsnips are cooked through and the crab is warmed. Serve hot, garnished with parsley and pea shoots.

2 tablespoons olive oil

2 medium garlic cloves, finely chopped

¼ teaspoon crushed dried chillies

2 large parsnips, peeled, spiralized with
   BLADE C

Salt and pepper

225g jumbo lump white crabmeat, fresh
   if possible

1 tablespoon fresh lemon juice

Finely chopped fresh parsley

25g pea shoots

The gentle flavour of true crab is what elevates this recipe; imitation won't work nearly as well. While premium jumbo lump crab is best, regular lump will also do the trick.

If you're not wheat-free, serve this dish with crusty warmed wholegrain or Italian bread to sop up the sauce.

Courgette Linguine with Garlic Clam Sauce

MAKES
3–4 servings

GF

P

TIME TO PREPARE
20 minutes

TIME TO COOK
25 minutes

NUTRITIONAL INFORMATION
SERVING SIZE: 1/4 **recipe**
Calories: 237
Fat: 8g
Carbohydrates: 20g
Salt: 2.7g
Protein: 20g
Sugar: 4g

ALSO WORKS WELL WITH
Kohlrabi • Butternut
Squash • Parsnips •
Swedes • Celeriac

My favourite pasta meal growing up was my mother's garlic crab spaghetti. The ingredients were so modest, yet the flavours so vivid. As I got older and started eating out on my own, I discovered clam sauce. Clams have that same light seafood taste, but also have a more intense seafood flavour, which is absorbed by the courgette noodles in this dish. The garlic clam sauce is wonderful on a hot summer night when you're surrounded by friends and loved ones – it will bring everyone back to the basics.

1 Place a large saucepan over a medium heat and add the olive oil. When the oil is shimmering, add the garlic and shallots. Cook for 2–3 minutes or until shallots are translucent. Add the crushed dried chillies, reserved clam juice, and wine, and season with salt and pepper. Increase the heat to high, bring to the boil, then reduce the heat to low. Simmer until the sauce is reduced by about half.

2 Add the fresh clams to the sauce and cover. Steam for 7–10 minutes. Discard any that don't open after 10 minutes, then add the chopped clams. Stir in the courgette noodles and 1 tablespoon of the parsley. Cook for 2–3 minutes or until the courgette noodles are *al dente*.

3 Divide the pasta among bowls and garnish with the remaining tablespoon parsley, the pepper, and the lemon wedges.

2 tablespoons olive oil

2 garlic cloves, finely chopped

2 medium shallots, finely chopped

Pinch of crushed dried chillies

400g tinned chopped clams, drained, with half the juice reserved

120ml dry white wine (such as Sauvignon Blanc)

Salt and pepper

675g littleneck or other small fresh clams, rinsed and scrubbed

3 large courgettes, spiralized with BLADE C

2 tablespoons finely chopped fresh parsley

Freshly cracked black peppercorns

2 lemons, quartered

Halibut en Papillote with Butternut Squash

MAKES
4 servings

GF

P

TIME TO PREPARE
20 minutes

TIME TO COOK
15 minutes

NUTRITIONAL INFORMATION
SERVING SIZE: ¼ **recipe**
Calories: 323
Fats: 13g
Carbohydrates: 22g
Salt: 0.5g
Protein: 30g
Sugar: 3g

One of the first meals I ever made for Lu was a fish *en papillote,* or in parchment – a preparation that sounds really fancy and complex, but is the exact opposite. It's impressive nonetheless (that's why I made it!). The juices from the halibut seep into the butternut squash noodles and steam them, locking in the flavour. When you open your parchment pouch, the aromatics are elegant and everything is cooked to perfection.

1 Preheat the oven to 200°C/400°F. In a large bowl, toss together the butternut squash noodles, olive oil, leeks, garlic, and olives. Season with pepper.

2 Lay out four large pieces of parchment paper, about 25cm square. In the centre of each, place some of the squash noodle mixture. Top with a halibut piece and drizzle each with 1 tablespoon lemon juice. Add 2 thyme sprigs to each bundle and season with salt and pepper.

3 Seal the parchment packets by crimping the edges together to make a pouch, folding over once. Place on a baking tray and bake for 10–13 minutes. Place the packets on plates, slit open, and serve.

1 small butternut squash, peeled and bulbous end removed, spiralized with **BLADE C**

2 tablespoons olive oil

60g leeks, thinly sliced

2 medium garlic cloves, thinly sliced

50g pitted green olives, halved

Salt and black pepper

4 (115g) pieces of halibut fillet, skin removed

60ml fresh lemon juice

8 fresh thyme sprigs

All spiralized vegetables bake well in parchment except for cucumber noodles (they're too wet).

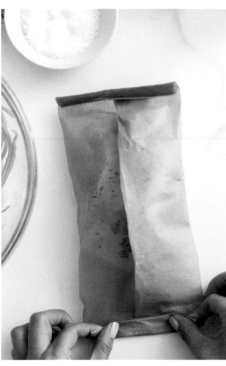

Bikini Bolognese

MAKES
2 servings

GF

TIME TO PREPARE
20 minutes

TIME TO COOK
25 minutes

NUTRITIONAL INFORMATION
SERVING SIZE: 1/2 **recipe**
Calories: 285
Fat: 11g
Carbohydrates: 31g
Salt: 1.1g
Protein: 21g
Sugar: 6g

ALSO WORKS WELL WITH
Kohlrabi • Sweet
Potatoes • Carrots •
Beets • Butternut
Squash • Swedes •
Celeriac

I'd like to think I live life with no regrets, but there might be one exception. When my family and I arrived in Rome on a holiday together, after a long day of travelling, my father used room service to order his favourite pasta dish: rigatoni and bolognese. I wasn't eating meat at the time, so I just watched as my entire family dived in. To this day I remember that giant ceramic bowl of thick rigatoni and how the aroma filled the room. Clearly, I wasn't following the "when in Rome" mantra. This recipe is an Italian classic and belongs in your arsenal.

1 Place the celery and carrot in a food processor and pulse until finely chopped; the mixture should be somewhere between chunky and puréed.

2 In a large frying pan, heat the olive oil over a medium heat and season with salt and pepper. When the oil is shimmering, add the garlic and cook for 30 seconds or until fragrant. Add the crushed dried chillies and cook for 30 seconds. Then add the onion and cook for 1–2 minutes or until it begins to soften.

3 Add the carrot and celery mixture to the frying pan and cook for about 2 minutes or until it begins to soften. Push the veggie mixture to one side of the pan and add the turkey, breaking it up with a wooden spoon. Add a pinch of the oregano and cook until the turkey is browned. Then combine the vegetables with the turkey in the pan and season with another pinch of oregano.

½ celery stick, diced

½ medium carrot, diced

2 tablespoons olive oil

Salt and pepper

2 medium garlic cloves, finely chopped

1 teaspoon crushed dried chillies

½ medium red onion, chopped

225g turkey mince

1 tablespoon dried oregano

60ml reduced-salt chicken stock

400g tinned chopped tomatoes (such as San Marzano)

1 tablespoon tomato purée

15g fresh basil, chopped

2–2½ large courgettes, spiralized with BLADE C

Shavings of Parmesan cheese

4 Add the chicken stock and simmer until absorbed. Add the tomatoes and tomato purée, and season generously with salt and pepper. Sprinkle in the remaining oregano. Increase the heat to high and bring to the boil, then reduce the heat and simmer for 15 minutes.

5 Add the basil to the sauce and then add the courgette noodles, mixing thoroughly and cooking for 2–3 minutes or until the courgette noodles are *al dente*. Serve hot, sprinkled with Parmesan cheese.

If you like your bolognese extra-spicy, add more crushed dried chillies in step 2.

Albondigas and Courgettes with Tomato-Serrano Sauce

MAKES
4 servings

TIME TO PREPARE
25 minutes

TIME TO COOK
30 minutes

NUTRITIONAL INFORMATION
SERVING SIZE: $^{1}/_{4}$ **recipe**
Calories: 300
Fat: 14g
Carbohydrates: 11g
Salt: 0.9g
Protein: 29g
Sugar: 10g

ALSO WORKS WELL WITH
Turnips • Swedes •
Kohlrabi •
Celeriac • Sweet
Potatoes • Carrots

I've taken some of my favourite flavours and created a Latin-themed meatball (*albondiga*) dish, presented here with courgette noodles. It's an adaptation of my grandparents' traditional Italian dish, altered to fit a healthier lifestyle without sacrificing flavour.

For the albondigas
- 450g lean beef mince
- 30g yellow onion, diced
- 1 large garlic clove, finely chopped
- 1 teaspoon dried oregano
- 2½ tablespoons chopped fresh mint
- Salt and pepper

For the sauce
- 1 tablespoon olive oil
- 1 medium garlic clove, finely chopped
- 60g yellow onion, diced
- 2 serrano chillies, stems and seeds removed, diced
- 800g tinned chopped tomatoes
- Salt and pepper
- 2 tablespoons chopped fresh coriander
- 3 courgettes, spiralized with BLADE C

(recipe continues)

1 Make the albondigas. Preheat the oven to 190°C/375°F. Line a baking tray with parchment paper. Combine the ingredients for the albondigas in a large bowl. Using your hands, form 8–10 meatballs about 2.5cm in diameter and space them evenly on the baking tray. Bake for 18–20 minutes or until browned, flipping them over halfway through.

2 Prepare the sauce. Add the olive oil to a large saucepan or pot over a medium heat. When the oil is shimmering, add the garlic and cook for 30 seconds or until fragrant. Add the onion and chillies, and cook for 2–3 minutes or until the onion is translucent. Add the tomatoes, season with salt and pepper, and crush the tomatoes using a potato masher or the back of a fork. Increase the heat to high and bring to the boil. Add the coriander, reduce the heat to low, and simmer for 10–15 minutes or until the sauce thickens, stirring occasionally.

3 Add the meatballs to the sauce and continue to simmer, turning to coat them, for 1–2 minutes. Scoop out the meatballs and set aside, then add the courgette noodles to the sauce. Toss to combine thoroughly and cook for 3 minutes or until courgette noodles are *al dente*.

4 Serve the noodles warm, topped with the meatballs, and with any extra sauce spooned over.

Thai Drunken Courgette Noodles with Pork

~~~ | MAKES
2 servings

TIME TO PREPARE
15 minutes

TIME TO COOK
20 minutes

NUTRITIONAL INFORMATION
SERVING SIZE: ½ **recipe**
Calories: 383
Fat: 22g
Carbohydrates: 18g
Salt: 3.5g
Protein: 27g
Sugar: 10g

Family and friends often ask me, "Are you ever stumped for recipe ideas?" I usually feel the opposite: I never know which recipes to try first because my 'to make' list is pages long! But I also like to create the noodle classics – lo mein, spaghetti alfredo, and so on. I've finally created a version of Thai drunken noodles that uses flat courgette noodles instead of wide rice noodles and has no added sugars.

1 Heat a large non-stick frying pan over a medium heat. When a bit of water flicked onto the frying pan sizzles, add the hoisin sauce, soy sauce, oyster sauce, chilli oil, and fish sauce. When the sauces have heated and combined for about 2 minutes, transfer to a bowl.

2 Add the coconut oil to the same frying pan over a medium heat. When the oil is shimmering, add the pork and sauté, breaking up with a wooden spoon, for 5 minutes or until cooked through and browned. Add the shallots and garlic and cook 2–3 minutes more or until the shallots begin to brown.

3 Return the sauce mixture to the frying pan and add the red pepper and spring onions. Cook for 1 minute, stirring frequently. Add the courgette noodles and cook 2–3 minutes or until the courgette noodles soften. Fold in the Thai basil leaves and serve.

1 tablespoon hoisin sauce

1 tablespoon reduced-salt soy sauce

½ tablespoon oyster sauce

1 tablespoon Thai chilli oil

1 tablespoon Thai or Vietnamese fish sauce

1 tablespoon virgin coconut oil

225g pork mince

2 small shallots, finely chopped

1 medium garlic clove, finely chopped

1 small red pepper, sliced into strips

2 spring onions, green and white parts, thinly sliced

2 medium courgettes, spiralized with **BLADE A**

3 tablespoons chopped fresh Thai basil leaves

Drunken noodles are meant to be spicy, so if you can't find Thai chilli oil, use Sriracha or a chilli garlic sauce.

Vegan Celeriac Alfredo with Tenderstem Broccoli

MAKES
4 servings

GF

TIME TO PREPARE
20 minutes

V

TIME TO COOK
20 minutes

P

NUTRITIONAL INFORMATION
SERVING SIZE: ¼ **recipe**
Calories: 155
Fat: 7g
Carbohydrates: 19g
Salt: 1.4g
Protein: 7g
Sugar: 6g

ALSO WORKS WELL WITH
Swedes • Courgettes •
Sweet Potatoes •
Butternut Squash •
Kohlrabi • Turnips •
Parsnips

This vegan alfredo has a go-to sauce that works with any vegetable pasta. In this version, the earthy taste of the celeriac noodles, the warm tenderness of the tenderstem broccoli, and the alfredo consistency from the cauliflower encapsulate everything *Inspiralized* is about: eating nutritious and energizing food. You'll feel like you're in Italy, twisting forkfuls of a creamy bowl of indulgence.

1 Place the cauliflower florets in a large pot and cover with salted water. Bring to the boil over a high heat, then lower the heat to medium and cook for 5–7 minutes or until easily pierced with a fork. Remove the cauliflower with a slotted spoon.

2 With the water still boiling, add the tenderstem broccoli and cook for 2 minutes or until firm-tender. Fill a medium bowl with ice cubes. Drain the tenderstem broccoli and immediately place in the ice water to stop the cooking. Pat dry and then slice off the florets. Chop the stems into 2.5cm pieces.

Florets from 1 small-to-medium cauliflower

2 bunches tenderstem broccoli (about 2.5cm of tough stems trimmed)

2 tablespoons olive oil

2 medium garlic cloves, finely chopped

2 tablespoons finely chopped shallots

480ml reduced-salt vegetable stock

1½ tablespoons nutritional yeast

½ teaspoon Dijon mustard

4 teaspoons fresh lemon juice

Salt and pepper

Pinch of crushed dried chillies

2 large celeriac knobs, peeled, spiralized with **BLADE C**

2 tablespoons finely chopped fresh parsley

(recipe continues)

3 Heat 1 tablespoon of the olive oil in a medium non-stick frying pan over a medium heat. When the oil is shimmering, add one chopped garlic clove and cook for 30 seconds or until fragrant. Add the shallots and cook for 2–3 minutes or until translucent. Transfer to a high-speed blender or large food processor, and add the cauliflower, the vegetable stock, nutritional yeast, mustard, and lemon juice. Generously season with salt and pepper and blend the sauce until creamy, about 1 minute.

4 Return the tenderstem broccoli pot to a medium heat and add the remaining 1 tablespoon olive oil. When the oil is shimmering, add the remaining garlic and the crushed dried chillies. Cook for 30 seconds or until fragrant, then add the tenderstem broccoli florets and stems. Add the celeriac noodles. Season generously with salt and pepper, cover, and cook for 5–7 minutes, tossing occasionally, until the noodles are *al dente*. Transfer the noodles and vegetables to a serving bowl.

5 Place a medium frying pan over a medium-low heat and add the cauliflower sauce. Simmer to heat through, at least 5 minutes. Stir in the parsley, then pour the sauce over the noodles. Toss to combine and serve warm.

It's essential to lightly boil the tenderstem broccoli first to minimize its bitterness. A quick blanch will highlight its robust, grassy, and slightly sweet flavour.

Sweet Potato Carbonara

MAKES
4 servings

GF

TIME TO PREPARE
15 minutes

TIME TO COOK
15 minutes

NUTRITIONAL INFORMATION
SERVING SIZE: ¼ recipe
Calories: 345
Fat: 22g
Carbohydrates: 21g
Salt: 1.8g
Protein: 14g
Sugar: 9g

The sweet potato noodles work well in this dish because they soak up the egg and really transform this carbonara sauce with their natural sugars. The pancetta adds savoury balance. Consider this pasta a slightly sweeter, more colourful, and cleaner version of the original.

1 Heat a large non-stick frying pan over a medium heat and coat with cooking spray. When some water flicked onto the frying pan sizzles, add the sweet potato noodles and cook for 5–7 minutes, tossing frequently, until softened and lightly browned.

2 Heat the olive oil over a medium heat in a separate large non-stick frying pan. When the oil is shimmering, add the garlic and crushed dried chillies. Cook for 30 seconds, stirring frequently, until fragrant, then add the onion. Cook for 2–3 minutes or until the onion begins to soften. Add the pancetta, stirring frequently until cooked through, about 5 minutes more.

3 Whisk together the eggs and cheese in a medium bowl until smooth. Season with the salt and pepper.

4 Add the sweet potato noodles to the frying pan with the pancetta, toss to combine, then turn off the heat. Slowly pour the egg-cheese mixture over the noodles, stirring constantly to cook the eggs and coat the noodles. Serve hot.

Cooking spray

2 large sweet potatoes, peeled, spiralized with BLADE C

2 tablespoons olive oil

2 medium garlic cloves, finely chopped

¼ teaspoon crushed dried chillies

½ medium red onion, diced

225g pancetta, diced

2 medium eggs

30g Parmesan cheese, grated

Salt and pepper

If you can't find pancetta at your supermarket, you can substitute bacon.

If you don't like your tuna rare, cook it for an extra 2-3 minutes on each side.

Seared Tuna with Chimichurri

MAKES
2 servings

GF

P

TIME TO PREPARE
20 minutes

TIME TO COOK
10 minutes

NUTRITIONAL INFORMATION
SERVING SIZE: 1/2 **recipe**
Calories: 360
Fat: 22g
Carbohydrates: 14g
Salt: 0.1g
Protein: 27g
Sugar: 3g

My friend Jen, who studied at Le Cordon Bleu in Paris, was in a cooking competition on television and had to make just one dish to wow the judges. When she was preparing for the show, she invited me for a recipe testing. One of the options was a dish elegantly drizzled with a chimichurri sauce. I never forgot the freshness of it and I set out to duplicate it in my own way. Here, it works wonders on these light cucumber noodles and quick-seared tuna.

1 Combine all the chimichurri ingredients in a food processor and pulse until creamy.

2 Season the tuna fillets generously with salt and pepper on both sides, pressing to adhere. Heat the olive oil in a large non-stick frying pan over a medium heat. When the oil is shimmering, add the tuna and cook for 1–1½ minutes per side, adding the lime juice after you flip them. Remove the tuna from the frying pan and slice into slice into strips, approximately 1.5cm wide.

3 Remove the noodles from the fridge, drizzle over the chimichurri, and then top with the tuna. Drizzle additional chimichurri on top and serve.

For the chimichurri
15g fresh flat-leaf parsley
½ teaspoon dried oregano
15g fresh coriander
2 medium garlic cloves, finely chopped
½ serrano chilli or jalapeño pepper, deseeded and diced
2 tablespoons diced white onion
1½ tablespoons red wine vinegar
2 tablespoons olive oil
Salt and pepper

2 (115g) yellowfin tuna fillets
Salt and cracked black peppercorns
1 tablespoon olive oil
2 tablespoons fresh lime juice
1 large seedless cucumber, spiralized with BLADE C OR BLADE D, patted dry and chilled

Pesto Turnips with Shredded Brussels Sprouts

MAKES
3 servings

GF

V

P

TIME TO PREPARE
15 minutes

TIME TO COOK
15 minutes

NUTRITIONAL INFORMATION
SERVING SIZE: ⅓ **recipe**
Calories: 310
Fat: 26g
Carbohydrates: 17g
Salt: 0.3g
Protein: 4g
Sugar: 8g

ALSO WORKS WELL WITH
Parsnips • Courgettes
• Swedes • Butternut
Squash • Beetroot •
Celeriac

Turnips can be tricky because they have a distinct radish-like taste. In this recipe, we toss the warm turnip noodles with a robust pesto, thereby enjoying the root vegetable while masking most of its bitterness. The Brussels sprouts offer an almost velvety softness; they also pack a hearty amount of vitamin C, which is an important nutrient during those cold winter months. Keep healthy and curl up with this warm, flavourful pasta.

1 Make the pesto. Combine the basil, pine nuts, olive oil, garlic, salt, and pepper in a food processor and pulse until smooth.

2 Halve and then thinly slice the Brussels sprouts to shreds.

3 Heat the olive oil in a large frying pan over a medium heat. When the oil is shimmering, add the turnip noodles and Brussels sprouts, and season with salt and pepper. Cover and cook for 3–5 minutes or until the turnip noodles are *al dente*, uncovering and tossing occasionally. Transfer to a large bowl. Pour the pesto on top and toss to combine thoroughly. Serve warm.

100g basil leaves

2 tablespoons pine nuts

60ml olive oil

1 large garlic clove, finely chopped

½ teaspoon freshly ground sea salt

¼ teaspoon freshly ground black pepper

200g trimmed Brussels sprouts

1 tablespoon extra-virgin olive oil

3 medium turnips, peeled, spiralized with BLADE C

Salt and pepper

Try turning this basil pesto into a coriander pesto and use pepitas (Mexican pumpkin seeds) instead of pine nuts.

Tofu Miso-Tahini Carrot Bowl

MAKES
2 servings

TIME TO PREPARE
15 minutes

TIME TO COOK
15 minutes

NUTRITIONAL INFORMATION
SERVING SIZE: ½ **recipe**
Calories: 494
Fat: 36g
Carbohydrates: 28g
Salt: 4g
Protein: 21g
Sugar: 10g

ALSO WORKS WELL WITH
Courgettes • Kohlrabi •
Broccoli

Tofu is like a sponge; it absorbs flavours very well. One of my favourite ways to prepare tofu is to marinate it in soy sauce and then roast it, as in this recipe. When I was vegan, my go-to dinner was roasted tofu with brown rice and a sautéed vegetable medley. BOR-ing! This meal is much more exciting, but with that same easy tofu. With the thick dressing, the carrot noodles soften slightly and combine with the miso and tahini, while the edamame beans offer a lean protein and a colourful crunch. This works for lunch or dinner, and also stores well in the fridge.

1 Make the dressing. Pulse the ingredients in a food processor until creamy. If necessary, add water a teaspoon at a time until the dressing reaches the desired consistency.

2 Line a plate with two layers of kitchen paper. Place the tofu cubes on top of the kitchen paper and add two more layers of kitchen paper. Gently press down on the tofu, removing excess moisture. Repeat with fresh kitchen paper.

3 Preheat the oven to 200°C/400°F. Coat a baking tray with cooking spray. Place the tofu in a medium bowl with the soy sauce, tossing to coat. Transfer to the baking tray and roast for 10–13 minutes or until lightly browned.

For the dressing
6 tablespoons tahini
2 tablespoons fresh lemon juice
2 tablespoons miso paste
1 tablespoon vegetable oil
1 teaspoon finely chopped garlic
2 teaspoons mirin
Salt and pepper

60g firm tofu, cubed
2 tablespoons reduced-salt soy sauce
Cooking spray
2 large carrots, peeled, spiralized with **BLADE C OR BLADE D**
40g frozen edamame beans
1 teaspoon white sesame seeds
4 tablespoons sunflower sprouts

4 Place a medium saucepan of water over a high heat and bring to the boil. Add the carrot noodles and edamame beans, and cook for 2 minutes or until *al dente*. Drain well.

5 Place a small frying pan over a medium-high heat. When a little water flicked onto the frying pan sizzles, add the sesame seeds and cook for 2–3 minutes, tossing frequently until aromatic and just beginning to brown.

6 In a large bowl, combine the edamame beans and carrot noodles, and add the sunflower sprouts. Toss with the dressing and top with the tofu and sesame seeds.

If you can't find sunflower sprouts, substitute watercress or pea shoots.

DESSERTS

Pecan and Carrot Almond Butter Bars with Chocolate Drizzle

Pear Rhubarb Crisp

Apple Ambrosia Fruit Salad

No-Bake Plantain Cacao Balls

Plantain Coconut Rice Pudding

Apple and Pear Ricotta Parfaits with Pistachios

Double Chocolate-Pecan Sweet Potato Dessert Pancakes

Blueberry Pear Ice Lollies

Chocolate Chip Sweet Potato Muffins

Pecan and Carrot Almond Butter Bars with Chocolate Drizzle

MAKES
8–10 bars

GF

TIME TO PREPARE
30 minutes

V

NUTRITIONAL INFORMATION
SERVING SIZE: 1 bar
Calories: 316
Fat: 26g
Carbohydrates: 19g
Salt: 0.2g
Protein: 10g
Sugar: 11g

P

One of the oldest tricks in the book of healthy eating is to always be prepared. By stocking your fridge and pantry with nutritious snacks, you're ahead of the game simply because you have no other choice but to eat healthy when you're hungry. These dessert bars have it all: chocolate, crunchy nuts, creamy almond butter, and even some fruit and veggies.

1 Line an 28 x 18cm baking tin with parchment paper.

2 In a large bowl, combine the carrot rice, almond butter, maple syrup, pecans, sultanas, and a pinch of salt and mix thoroughly.

3 Transfer the carrot rice mixture to the baking tin and spread in an even layer. Top with clingfilm and use your hands to press down so that the mixture is uniformly flat, about 2.5cm thick. Remove the clingfilm.

4 Make the drizzle. In a small saucepan over a medium heat, melt the chocolate chips with the almond milk, whisking continually until the chocolate is melted. If the sauce is too thick, add a bit more milk, 1 tablespoon at a time.

5 Drizzle the chocolate over the carrot rice mixture. Place the baking tin in the freezer for at least 4 hours. While still frozen, cut into bars. Store refrigerated in an airtight container and serve cold.

2 large carrots, peeled, spiralized with **BLADE C**, then riced (see page 25)

225g smooth almond butter

1 tablespoon pure maple syrup

60g whole pecans, roughly chopped

45g sultanas

Pinch of salt

For the chocolate drizzle
80g dairy-free chocolate chips
2 tablespoons almond milk

The bars are easily adaptable to suit your taste; try making them with other nuts, such as almonds and walnuts, or other nut butters, such as hazelnut and peanut.

Pear Rhubarb Crisp

MAKES
4 servings

TIME TO PREPARE
15 minutes

TIME TO COOK
30 minutes

NUTRITIONAL INFORMATION
SERVING SIZE: 1 ramekin
Calories: 142
Fat: 2g
Carbohydrates: 32g
Salt: 0.1g
Protein: 3g
Sugar: 16g

ALSO WORKS WELL WITH
Apples

Rhubarb is used primarily in baking, yielding an impeccable natural tartness that pairs well with sweet fruit. The combination with pear here is remarkable. And what's the best part of this recipe? You don't have to stand at your kitchen counter, painstakingly slicing the pear with a mandoline or knife – the spiralizer simplifies the process. You'll need four 10 x 4.5cm ramekins for this preparation.

1 Preheat the oven to 180°C/350°F. Coat the inside of four 10 x 4.5cm ramekins with cooking spray.

2 Slice the rhubarb, then dice. In a large bowl, toss the rhubarb with the pear noodles, cinnamon, orange juice, and zest.

3 Pack the mixture into the ramekins, filling each three-quarters full. Set the ramekins on a baking sheet and bake for 30 minutes or until the noodles wilt.

4 Top each ramekin with 2 tablespoons of granola and return them to the oven to bake for another 5 minutes. Serve immediately.

Cooking spray

450g rhubarb

3 pears, spiralized with BLADE C

1 teaspoon ground cinnamon

3 tablespoons fresh orange juice

Zest of ½ orange

60g gluten-free granola

Apple Ambrosia Fruit Salad

MAKES
4 servings

GF

TIME TO PREPARE
20 minutes

VT

P

NUTRITIONAL INFORMATION
SERVING SIZE: 1/4 **recipe**
Calories: 356
Fat: 29g
Carbohydrates: 22g
Salt: 0.1g
Protein: 4g
Sugar: 17g

The summer after I turned vegan, I was living in New York City. One hot day I went on a quest for vegan "ice cream" and found a spot with a sign in the window that read "Dairy Free Organic Yogurt". I came out victorious: a cup of coconut frozen yogurt topped with chunks of apple and pineapple. Although I'm more of a cake person now than an ice cream one, I still dream about those fresh flavours I tasted that day and have re-created them here.

1 Cut the apple vertically halfway to the centre, being sure not to pierce the centre. Spiralize using blade B.

2 Scoop off the top layer of 'cream' from the coconut milk and put into a medium bowl. (Discard the remainder or save for another use.) Add the vanilla extract, orange juice, and honey and whisk until light and foamy. Add the pineapple, pecans, coconut, and apple noodles and stir thoroughly to combine. Chill in the fridge until ready to serve.

1 apple (Gala, or other sweet variety)

420ml full-fat coconut milk, refrigerated for 24 hours

1 teaspoon vanilla extract

2 tablespoons orange juice

2 teaspoons honey

125g diced pineapple

105g chopped pecans

25g unsweetened coconut flakes

If you're serving this fruit salad at a party, divide it among sundae glasses and garnish with maraschino cherries. Also, note that the apples will absorb more flavour the longer they sit.

No-Bake Plantain Cacao Balls

MAKES
10–12 balls

TIME TO PREPARE
20 minutes

TIME TO COOK
5 minutes

NUTRITIONAL INFORMATION
SERVING SIZE: 1 ball
Calories: 120
Fat: 1g
Carbohydrates: 30g
Salt: 0g
Protein: 1g
Sugar: 21g

Having unprocessed sweets and snacks in your house is the key to balanced eating. If you stock your pantry and fridge with clean treats, your body and mind will thank you and your mind-set will shift away from "following a diet" and towards living a lifestyle. These easy, no-bake balls are exactly that – made with real, whole ingredients, and only five of them. They won't give you a sugar crash, and the plantain's starchiness helps bind everything and keep you fuelled longer. Snack on these no-bake balls to satisfy your sweet tooth and give you that energy boost.

1 Place a large non-stick frying pan over a medium-high heat. When a little water flicked onto the frying pan sizzles, add the plantain rice and cook for 3 minutes, tossing frequently, until browned. Remove the pan from the heat and set aside.

2 Pulse the dates in a food processor until paste-like, about 1 minute. If the dates don't break down easily, add a little water, 1 teaspoon at a time. Add the plantain rice, the cacao powder, and coconut flakes and continue to pulse until the mixture is sticky and smooth.

3 Transfer the mixture to a medium bowl and add the pepitas, mixing by hand until blended well. Form 10–12 balls that are 2.5cm in diameter and refrigerate for at least 15 minutes before serving.

2 plantains, peeled, spiralized with BLADE C, then riced (see page 25)

10 Medjool dates, stoned and roughly chopped

2 teaspoons raw cacao powder

1½ tablespoons unsweetened coconut flakes

1 tablespoon roasted and salted pepitas (Mexican pumpkin seeds)

Plantain Coconut Rice Pudding

MAKES
1 serving

GF

V

P

TIME TO PREPARE
15 minutes

TIME TO COOK
10 minutes

NUTRITIONAL INFORMATION
SERVING SIZE: 1 recipe quantity
Calories: 476
Carbohydrates: 112g
Salt: 0.5g
Protein: 5g
Sugar: 71g

I never liked rice pudding until I met this recipe. Here, the coconut meshes organically with the slight sweetness of the plantain and the creaminess of the almond milk, hence a warm balance results. The raisins and cinnamon invoke that classic rice pudding aroma and flavour, too. Everything comes together in this lightened version of the classic, now a simple vegan dessert that's ideal for an after-dinner treat.

1 In a medium saucepan over a high heat, combine the plantain rice and 250ml of the almond milk. Bring to the boil, then lower the heat and simmer for 10 minutes or until the liquid reduces to the point that the rice begins to stick to the bottom of the pan. Add the remaining 75ml almond milk and simmer to reduce again, stirring occasionally until the mixture is creamy, about 3 minutes.

2 Remove the pan from the heat and add the cinnamon, coconut flakes, and raisins. Stir until the cinnamon dissolves into the pudding. Serve hot.

1 medium-ripe plantain, peeled, spiralized with BLADE C, then riced (see page 25)

325ml vanilla almond milk

⅛ teaspoon ground cinnamon

1–2 teaspoons unsweetened coconut flakes

35g raisins

If you don't have access to vanilla almond milk or prefer to use a milk type that's not flavoured, just add 1 teaspoon vanilla extract to the mix.

Apple and Pear Ricotta Parfaits with Pistachios

MAKES
2 servings

TIME TO PREPARE
10 minutes

NUTRITIONAL INFORMATION
SERVING SIZE: ¹/₂ **recipe**
Calories: 485
Fat: 19g
Carbohydrates: 75g
Salt: 0.5g
Protein: 14g
Sugar: 58g

Every time I see a parfait at a coffee shop or supermarket, I cringe. They look so lifeless! There's never been anything special about them – until now. These fruit noodles are fresh and crunchy; the ricotta whipped with honey and vanilla adds a creamy, sweet consistency.

1 In a medium bowl, whisk together the ricotta, honey, and vanilla extract until light and fluffy.

2 Evenly divide the raspberry jam into two parfait or dessert glasses. Layer on the ricotta, and add the apple and pear noodles. Sprinkle the pistachios on top and serve immediately.

110g ricotta cheese

2 tablespoons honey

1 teaspoon vanilla extract

75g raspberry jam

1 apple, spiralized with BLADE C

1 pear, spiralized with BLADE C

60g pistachios, roughly chopped, roasted and salted

Convert this dessert parfait into a breakfast parfait by swapping natural 0% fat Greek yogurt for the ricotta.

Double Chocolate–Pecan Sweet Potato Dessert Pancakes

MAKES
2 pancakes

TIME TO PREPARE
20 minutes

TIME TO COOK
15 minutes

NUTRITIONAL INFORMATION
SERVING SIZE: 1 pancake
Calories: 381
Fat: 24g
Carbohydrates: 34g
Salt: 0.2g
Protein: 9g
Sugar: 18g

More often than not, when I go out for brunch I face a mental struggle: *Do I get the cinnamon swirl French toast with chocolate drizzle or the egg white scramble?* Nine times out of ten I make the healthy choice – but that one other time I enjoy every last bite of the indulgence. With these pancakes made from sweet potatoes, though, I don't have to struggle! Not only are they clean-eating friendly, but they're also satisfying – the natural sugar in the sweet potatoes is released and creates a pancake that's seemingly decadent *and* miraculously nutritious. Everyone loves breakfast for dinner, so why not make breakfast for dessert?

1 Place a large non-stick frying pan over a medium heat and coat with cooking spray. When a little water flicked onto the frying pan sizzles, add the sweet potato noodles and cover. Cook, turning occasionally, for 5 to 7 minutes or until the sweet potato noodles have softened and are lightly browned.

2 Combine the strawberries, pecans, honey, and yogurt in a medium bowl. Place in the fridge to briefly chill.

3 Transfer the sweet potato noodles to a large bowl and add the cacao powder, egg, vanilla extract, and chocolate chips. Toss to blend well.

Cooking spray

1 large sweet potato, peeled, spiralized with BLADE C

2 fresh strawberries, hulled and chopped

25g roughly chopped pecans

2 teaspoons honey

3 tablespoons natural 0% fat Greek yogurt

1 tablespoon raw cacao powder

1 medium egg, lightly beaten

1 teaspoon vanilla extract

2 tablespoons dairy-free dark chocolate chips

1 tablespoon olive oil

4 Return the frying pan to a medium heat and add half the olive oil. When the oil is shimmering, add half the sweet potato mixture to the centre of the frying pan. Using a spatula, quickly flatten into a pancake. Cook for about 2 minutes or until the bottom is set, then flip the pancake over, flatten again with a spatula, and cook for 2 minutes more or until completely set. Transfer to a plate. Repeat with remaining ½ tablespoon olive oil and remaining pancake mix.

5 Top the pancakes with the strawberry-yogurt mixture and serve.

If you prefer, you can easily turn these pancakes into dessert waffles simply by packing the noodle mixture into a waffle iron.

Blueberry Pear Ice Lollies

MAKES
10 ice lollies

GF

TIME TO PREPARE
8 hours+

VT

NUTRITIONAL INFORMATION
SERVING SIZE: **1 ice lolly**
Calories: 41
Fat: 0
Carbohydrates: 10g
Salt: 0g
Protein: 1g
Sugar: 7g

I have always preferred yogurts with real chunks of fruit at the bottom. After all, clean eating is all about consuming foods as close to whole as possible. So ditch the commercial ice lollies that are made with juice concentrate, and make these amazing yogurt ones that present a real fruit surprise. When the lolly starts to melt, the pear noodles pop through!

1 Place the yogurt, blueberries, and honey in a food processor and pulse until creamy. Trim the pear noodles so that they are no more than 10cm long.

2 For each ice lolly mould, put in a thin layer of pear noodles and then cover with some blueberry filling. Add another thin layer of pear noodles, pushing the noodles down into the yogurt mixture.

3 Insert the ice lolly sticks and freeze for at least 8 hours. To release the ice lollies from the mould, very briefly run each mould under hot water.

225g vanilla 0% fat Greek yogurt

125g fresh blueberries

1 tablespoon honey

2 ripe pears, peeled, spiralized with **BLADE C OR BLADE D**

If you don't have ice lolly moulds and sticks on hand, you can still make this dessert. Fill a shot glass or small cup with the filling, insert a sturdy straw in the centre, and freeze.

Chocolate Chip Sweet Potato Muffins

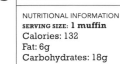

MAKES
6 muffins

TIME TO PREPARE
10 minutes

TIME TO COOK
25 minutes

NUTRITIONAL INFORMATION
SERVING SIZE: **1 muffin**
Calories: 132
Fat: 6g
Carbohydrates: 18g
Salt: 0.3g
Protein: 3g
Sugar: 12g

I made these muffins for a road trip I was taking with friends from high school. When everyone had piled in and settled into the back seat of my car, I whipped these out. The muffins got thumbs-up all around! Flourless, moist, and chocolatey, they came to be my trusty after-dinner treat and they won't cause a sugar crash later.

1 Preheat the oven to 190°C/375°F. Coat a 6-hole muffin tin lightly with cooking spray.

2 Combine the sweet potato rice, cinnamon, bicarbonate of soda, coconut flakes, and a pinch of salt in a medium bowl. Add the egg and egg white, honey, and vanilla extract and mix thoroughly. Fold in the chocolate chips.

3 Spoon the batter into the holes, filling each three-quarters full. Bake for 23–25 minutes or until a knife inserted in the centre of a muffin comes out clean. Remove the muffins from the tin and allow to cool on a rack for 5 minutes before serving.

Cooking spray

1 small sweet potato, peeled, spiralized with **BLADE C**, then riced (see page 25)

½ teaspoon ground cinnamon

½ teaspoon bicarbonate of soda

2 tablespoons unsweetened coconut flakes

Pinch of salt

1 medium egg plus 1 egg white

2 tablespoons honey

½ teaspoon vanilla extract

5 tablespoons dairy-free chocolate chips

The muffins are more moist than regular muffins because they are flourless. To prevent wet bottoms, allow them to rest for at least 30 minutes before storing in an airtight container.

FRUITS
AND
VEGGIES
A TO Z

Apple

The best part about spiralizing this fruit is that each different type of apple yields a unique flavour. Some apples, like Gala, are sweeter and some, like Granny Smith, are more sour. Apples spiralize very easily – the only preparation required is removing the stem. If you find that the apple stops spiralizing halfway through, simply flip it around, secure from the other end, and continue.

IMPORTANT NUTRIENTS: vitamin C

Beetroot

Don't be afraid to stain your spiralizer with beetroot – just rinse and scrub it with soap and water immediately after use. When beetroot is turned into noodles, it roasts much faster than when it is whole, which makes it ideal for quick cooking. You can also spiralize roasted whole beetroot. Treat golden and red beetroot the same way – and their green tips can be incorporated alongside the noodles.

IMPORTANT NUTRIENTS: folate and manganese

Broccoli

Most are surprised by the fact that, yes, you can spiralize a broccoli stem. When buying a head of broccoli for spiralizing, make sure that the stem is as thick and long as possible, at least 4cm wide and 12.5–15cm long for best results. When you remove the florets from the stem when preparing to spiralize, it's important to not waste much of the stem. You can save the broccoli florets for another use, but using them in the recipe enhances the flavour of their stem's noodles.

IMPORTANT NUTRIENTS: vitamin C, potassium, and calcium

Butternut squash

When choosing butternut squashes for spiralizing, try your best to find those with a small bulbous bottom. Remember, you must always slice that part off, since it has a seedy core and cannot be spiralized. It won't go to waste, though – dice it into cubes and save it for another use. If your butternut squash is very large, halve it before loading it onto the spiralizer for best results. If the noodles stick together, carefully pull them apart afterwards.

IMPORTANT NUTRIENTS: vitamins A and C

Carrot

The toughest part of spiralizing carrots is finding those that are large enough. An ideal carrot diameter is 5cm. This vegetable's naturally sweet taste makes it perfect for light sauces as well as dishes with salty foods like feta cheese and olives. When boiled, carrots have a similar consistency to wholemeal pasta.

IMPORTANT NUTRIENTS: vitamin A and beta-carotene

Cabbage

Spiralizing a cabbage won't yield cabbage noodles, but it is an easier, quicker way to 'shred' the vegetable. There's no preparation required and by simply running it through the spiralizer, you'll have shredded cabbage, best for using in slaws and salads.

IMPORTANT NUTRIENTS: vitamins C and K

Celeriac

Celeriac – the root that celery grows on – has the same tart, herbal taste as the commonly eaten sticks. Celeriac really looks like it grows in the ground – it's lumpy, tough, and difficult to peel. Once peeled, it takes maximum effort in the spiralizer, but the noodles have an earthy freshness that's wonderful with thick sauces and heavy proteins.

IMPORTANT NUTRIENTS: vitamins C and K and phosphorus

Courgette

Courgettes are the most popularly spiralized vegetables for a reason. Their soft but firm flesh is ideal for that *al dente* pasta texture. They have a mild taste, perfect for pairing with light sauces and for being used in pasta salads. Their only downfall is their high water content, so when they hit a warm sauce, they release liquid that can cause an unpleasant watery consistency. To best avoid this, see page 27 for tips. If you can't find large courgettes out of season, use blade A to yield the most noodles possible.

IMPORTANT NUTRIENTS: manganese, vitamin C, and folates

Cucumber

Cucumbers, normally just diced or cubed and tossed in salads, take on a new life with the spiralizer. They release a lot of excess moisture, however, so they must be patted very dry after spiralizing and before they're incorporated into a recipe.

IMPORTANT NUTRIENTS: hydration and vitamin K

Kohlrabi

Kohlrabis come in two different variations – white and purple – but both have a similar creamy yellow-coloured flesh. While peeling a kohlrabi can be a little tricky, it spiralizes effortlessly. The greens can be cooked right alongside its spiralized noodles. Kohlrabis taste like a fresh, crunchy broccoli stem with a hint of cucumber and are very versatile.

IMPORTANT NUTRIENTS: fibre and vitamin C

Onion

The spiralizer can be used to shred onions, which is best for hashes or to make noodles for caramelizing, baking into onion rings, and for tossing into salads. Typically, sliced onions have a lighter, more subtle taste when spiralized into noodles. Any type of large onion can be used: yellow, white, sweet, or red.

IMPORTANT NUTRIENTS: biotin (a vitamin B type) and manganese

Parsnip

Parsnips have a wonderfully nutty and sweet flavour when cooked, ideal for gratins and bakes. They taper in shape, so look for one with a thick top, or one that is as uniform in shape as possible. Prior to loading the parsnip onto the spiralizer, slice off any part of the parsnip that is less than 2.5cm in diameter and save for another use.

IMPORTANT NUTRIENTS: vitamin C, fibre, and manganese

Pear

Like apples, pears spiralize easily and require only the removal of the stem as preparation. They have velvety smooth flesh that's wonderful when paired with whole grains or tough proteins, like steaks. Each type of pear has a different flavour; Bosc pears are softer than Concorde, for example, and have honey and vanilla hints, respectively.

IMPORTANT NUTRIENTS: fibre and vitamin C

Plantain

Plantains are the staple sources of carbohydrates for large populations in Asia, Africa, the Caribbean, and Central and South America. The toughest food to spiralize, plantains are a bit of a stretch. However, they are extremely flavourful and therefore ideal in desserts. Plantains can be peeled using a knife or a peeler, but be careful not to slice off too much flesh.

IMPORTANT NUTRIENTS: vitamins A and C and potassium

Potato

Russet, white, and yellow potatoes all work well in the spiralizer. With russet potatoes, some moisture will seep out and can stain the spiralizer, so be sure to clean the tool immediately after use.

IMPORTANT NUTRIENTS: vitamin C and potassium

Radish

Radishes, with their typically soapy and bitter taste and smell, are transformed when spiralized. They are best used in soups, since they offer a fantastic crunch and absorb the flavours in the stock, masking their bite. Daikons (Asian radishes) are typically thick and long, ideal for spiralizing. Small red radishes will work well too!

IMPORTANT NUTRIENTS: vitamin C, potassium, and folate

Swede

Also known as rutabagas or wax turnips, swedes spiralize into long, sturdy spirals. They tend to be large, so just one swede yields several servings of noodles. In the same family as turnips and cabbage, they are mild and become sweeter when cooked. Swedes are resilient and can withstand all types of sauces and cooking methods.

IMPORTANT NUTRIENTS: vitamin C and potassium

Sweet potato or yam

Sweet potatoes and yams have a distinct, sweet taste that comes through when used in pasta and noodle dishes. They absorb liquids, so they work well with heavy pasta sauces, like a *pomodoro*. Since their flesh is tough, it takes some elbow grease to spiralize them, but they're well worth it. Never boil sweet potato noodles, because they will break apart into pieces.

IMPORTANT NUTRIENTS: vitamins B_6 and C and iron

Turnip

Turnips are a root vegetable with a slightly bitter flavour that can easily be masked by distinct sauces and dressings, such as a pesto. When buying turnips for spiralizing, be sure to find large, round ones to yield better spirals. Sautéed turnip noodles have an *al dente* pasta-like consistency. Due to their high water content, turnips might need to be drained prior to being cooked as rice. Just use your hands to squeeze out the liquid.

IMPORTANT NUTRIENTS: vitamin C and calcium

Yuca or cassava root

The tremendously tough flesh of yuca makes it difficult to spiralize. Not only is it tricky to get enough leverage, but the noodles also come out slightly shredded and uneven. Once spiralized, yuca can be sautéed but will soften and may not hold well. It works in desserts with natural sugars and other sweet add-ons. If you're a yuca lover and want to spiralize it, please do, but because it's not an ideal candidate for spiralizing, I haven't included any yuca recipes in this cookbook.

IMPORTANT NUTRIENTS: potassium

Nutritional Information of Vegetable Noodles

All of this nutritional data was calculated using the USDA National Nutrient Database for Standard Reference.

	Calories (G)	Carbs (G)	Fat (G)	Protein (G)	Sugar (G)
Beetroot (medium)	64.5	15	0.3	2.4	10.5
Broccoli stem (large)	68	14	0.8	5.6	3.4
Butternut squash (large)	81	21.6	0.18	1.8	3.96
Carrot (large)	77.9	19	0.38	1.71	8.93
Celeriac (large)	86.52	18.54	0.618	3.09	3.296
Courgette (medium)	41.65	7.595	0.735	2.94	6.125
Cucumber (large)	30.4	6.84	0.19	1.14	3.23
Daikon radish (large)	34.2	7.6	0	1.9	5.7
Kohlrabi (medium)	71.82	15.96	0.266	4.522	6.916
Parsnip (large)	120	28.8	0.48	1.92	7.68
Plantain (large)	122	32	0.4	1.3	15
Swede (large)	62.7	14.85	0.33	1.815	7.425
Sweet potato (large)	141.9	33	0	2.64	6.93
Turnip (large)	60.2	12.9	0.215	1.935	8.17
White potato (large)	134.3	30.6	0.17	3.57	1.02

Noodle Yields and Sizes

Each noodle serving comes to about 150–265g cooked, depending on the vegetable or fruit.

	Vegetable/Fruit Size (G)	Noodle Yield (G)	Noodle Serving (G)
Apple (medium)	195	150	N/A
Beetroot (medium)	248	150	150
Broccoli stem (large)	352	200	200
Butternut squash (large)	2074	870	180
Carrot (large)	500	363	190
Celeriac (large)	573	475	206
Courgette (medium)	298	280	245
Cucumber (large)	398	300	190
Daikon radish (large)	601	500	190
	Vegetable/Fruit Size (G)	Noodle Yield (G)	Noodle Serving (G)
Kohlrabi (medium)	385	266	266
Onion (medium)	230	164	N/A

Parsnip (large)	251	160		160
Pear (medium)	304	215		N/A
Plantain (large)	340	155		155
Swede (large)	905	767		165
Sweet potato large)	407	335		135
Turnip (large)	320	215		215
White potato (large)	536	700		170

Best Practices for Spiralizing Fruit and Veggies

Veggie/Fruit	Prep	Raw or Cooked	Cook Method	Cook Time (min)	Best Served As	Best Blade
Apple	Remove stem.	Both	Bake at 200°C	10	Snack, dessert	A
			Sauté in skillet	6–7	Snack, dessert	A
			Raw	N/A	Salad add-on	C
Beetroot	Peel and slice off ends.	Both	Sauté in skillet	6–8	Pasta, noodles	C, D
			Boil	3–4	Pasta, noodles, soup	C, B
			Bake at 190°C	25–30	Crisps	A
			Simmer	6–8	Rice	C, B
			Bake at 220°C	5–10	Pasta, noodles	C
			Raw	N/A	Noodles, salad add-on, snack	C, D
Broccoli stem	Peel to make an even skin surface.	Cooked	Sauté in skillet	6–7	Pasta, noodles, snack	C, D
			Boil	2–3	Pasta, noodles, snack, soup	C, D
Butternut squash	Peel, slice off ends, and chop in half.	Cooked	Bake at 200°C	8–10	Pasta, noodles	C, D
			Sauté in skillet	10	Pasta, noodles, rice	C
			Bake at 190°C	25–30	Crisps	A
Cabbage	Remove outer layers and slice in half.	Raw or Cooked	Sauté in skillet	4–5	Hot salad, hash	A
			Raw	N/A	Salad add-on, slaw, soup	A

(continued)

Veggie/Fruit	Prep	Raw or Cooked	Cook Method	Cook Time (min)	Best Served As	Best Blade
Carrot	Peel, slice off ends, and chop in half.	Both	Boil	3–4	Pasta, noodles, soup	C, B, D
			Simmer	5–7	Pasta, noodles	C, B, D
			Bake at 220°C	10–15	Chips, crisps	A, B, C
			Simmer	7–10	Rice	C, D
			Bake at 200°C	10	Pasta, noodles	C, D
			Raw	N/A	Salad add-on, slaw	C, D
Celeriac	Chop off ends of the root, peel, and chop in half if large.	Cooked	Sauté in skillet	6–7	Pasta, noodles, bun	C, D
			Bake at 200°C	10–15	Pasta, noodles	C
			Simmer	6–7	Rice, soup	C
			Bake at 200°C	15	Chips, crisps	All
Courgette	Slice off ends and chop in half	Both	Sauté in skillet	2–3	Pasta, noodles	All
			Simmer	2	Noodles, soup	All
			Raw	N/A	Pasta, noodles, salad add-on, slaw	All
Cucumber	Slice off ends and chop in half and press in between kitchen paper to remove excess moisture.	Raw	Press in between kitchen paper to remove excess moisture	Can be served immediately	Noodles, salad add-ons, soup	All
Daikon radish	Peel, slice off ends, and chop in half.	Both	Sauté in skillet	6–7	Pasta, noodles, bun	C
			Simmer	5	Soup	B, C, D
			Simmer	6–7	Rice	C
			Raw	N/A	Salad add-on, noodles	C
Kohlrabi	Peel, slice off ends, and chop in half if large.	Both	Sauté in skillet	6–8	Pasta, noodles, bun	C, D
			Bake at 220°C	10–15	Chips, crisps	A, B
			Simmer	3–4	Soup	B, C, D
Onion	Peel the outer papery layers of skin and chop off the ends.	Both	Sauté in skillet	3–4	Addition to a stir-fry, salad, soup	A
			Bake at 220°C	15–20	Onion rings or chips	C
			Raw	N/A	Salad add-on, slaw, soup	A, D
Parsnip	Peel, slice off ends, and chop in half.	Cooked	Sauté in skillet	6–7	Pasta, noodles, bun	C, D
			Bake at 200°C	10–12	Pasta, noodles	C
			Simmer	6–7	Rice	C
			Bake at 220°C	15–20	Chips, crisps	A, B
Pear	Chop off the ends.	Both	Sauté in skillet	6–7	Snack, dessert	A
			Bake at 200°C	8–10	Snack, dessert	A
			Raw	N/A	Salad add-on	C

Veggie/Fruit	Prep	Raw or Cooked	Cook Method	Cook Time (min)	Best Served As	Best Blade
Plantain	Slice off the ends, peel, and chop in half.	Cooked	Simmer	6–7	Rice	C
			Bake at 220°C	15	Chips, crisps	All
Potato	Peel, slice off ends, and chop in half if large.	Cooked	Sauté in skillet	6–8	Pasta, noodles	C, D
			Simmer	5–7	Pasta, noodles	C, D
			Bake at 220°C	15–20	Chips, crisps	All
Swede	Peel, slice off ends, and chop in half.	Cooked	Sauté in skillet	6–8	Pasta, noodles, bun	C, D
			Simmer	5–7	Pasta, noodles, soup	C, D
			Simmer	7–10	Rice	C
			Bake at 220°C	15–20	Pasta, noodles	C, B
Sweet potato	Peel, slice off ends, and chop in half if large.	Cooked	Sauté in skillet	6–8	Pasta, noodles, bun	C, D
			Simmer	5–7	Pasta, noodles	C, D
			Bake at 220°C	10–15	Pasta, noodles	C, B
Turnip	Chop off ends of the root and peel.	Cooked	Sauté in skillet	6–7	Pasta, noodles, soup	C, D
			Bake at 200°C	10–12	Pasta, noodles	C
			Simmer	6–7	Rice	C, D

ACKNOWLEDGEMENTS

For my first twenty-six years, I was living a life that followed the 'appropriate' track: do well in school, go to a notable university, get a job after graduation, and build a career. A few months after my twenty-sixth birthday, I quit my job and took a leap of faith in pursuit of a dream to make the world a happier and healthier place with Inspiralized.com. Now, just less than two years later, I am publishing my first cookbook, at age twenty-seven. Pinch me, please!

Without the support and love around me, I would never have achieved such success, especially in such little time. I would still be dreaming – not doing – and for that, I am eternally grateful to the following people:

Leah Bhabha, thank you for testing every single recipe in this book, responding to my texts at all hours, and being a fellow lover of all foods. Since we spent the larger part of our summer indoors in my kitchen, I think we owe ourselves a trip to the beach!

To every single reader, follower, and lover of Inspiralized – thank you, thank you, thank you. Every single 'like' you've given me on Facebook, every blog post of mine you've retweeted, and every friend you've tagged on my Instagram has brought me here. I'm honoured that you've trusted me enough to bring my recipes into your home and among your friends and family. Thank you for being truly Inspiralized.

Amanda Englander, thank you for guiding me through the publishing process as my editor. Thanks for entertaining all of my questions (no matter how obvious the answers were) and expediting the publication of this book – I can't wait to see it sitting on a bookshelf, finally in stores. Of course, thanks to the entire Clarkson Potter team, who I consider to be pioneers, believing in me and Inspiralized at such an early stage. Thanks for bringing my message to the masses!

Alyssa Reuben, thanks for supporting me every step of the way and believing in this spiralizing movement before anyone truly cared. This book is a result of your faith in me, and I'm forever appreciative to have you as my agent. Here's to many more books! Special thanks to Evan and Marisa Richheimmer for connecting Alyssa and me – you two were my original supporters!

To the entire photography crew that made this cookbook gorgeous – I'm still stunned. Thank you to Evan Sung for your incredible ability to capture spiralized vegetables and fruits, and for your kind, composed attitude throughout the experience. Thanks to Chelsea Zimmer for styling the vegetable noodles better than I can and Kaitlyn DuRoss for styling not only the photos but also me (I'm still finding pins in my shirts!).

Felicia, thank you for helping me spread the word about Inspiralized from the very beginning. I'm proud of the caring and loving person you've become, and I can't thank you enough for being there when I needed to vent, helping me plan a wedding while this book came to fruition, and for being my lifelong best friend. You'll always be my 'little sister'.

Dad, thanks for teaching me there are no shortcuts in life: just hard work, commitment, and determination. Without that, I would still be sitting at a desk, working a job that didn't fulfil me. You are the hardest-working man I have ever known, and I am grateful for every lesson in life you ever taught me. I'm proud to join the family ranks as an entrepreneur!

Grandma Ida, I thank you each and every day for teaching me to love reading and writing. Thank you for spending the countless hours with me, studying the literary classics and helping me to understand the way words come together when I struggled. Your faith in education and knowledge has led me to this hopefully never-ending chapter of my life.

Mum, I could write for hundreds of pages about how thankful I am to have you in my life and never do you justice. There is no one in this world who encourages, supports, and believes in me as much as you do. Not only am I forever grateful to you for introducing me to spiralizing, but I'm thankful for the hours and hours we've talked about living a healthy lifestyle – despite falling off the wagon a few times! You're my best friend, and knowing that I can come to you and talk about anything is more valuable to me than anything else. You've helped me write this book even when you weren't there. Nothing makes me happier than making you proud – this cookbook is as much yours as it is mine. I love you.

Pops, not only do I thank you for every last flawless meatball you put on my plate, but I thank you for being as strong as you are. From walking countless miles in the snow to court Grandma in your twenties to winning a very scary battle with cancer, your love and passion for life has always inspired me to live one that exceeds expectations and puts a smile on my face – and hopefully, on yours. You're my first true love and you'll always be my Poppy.

Grandma Loretta (Grams), you're the life of the party, the brightest smile in the room (and the best dressed!), and the most compassionate woman. Your faith and confidence in those you love is inspirational, and although you always manage to burn the sweet potatoes at Thanksgiving, you are the adorable glue that holds everyone together.

And Lu. When this book hits shelves, we'll be four months away from becoming husband and wife. You're the love of my life, and without you, the whole idea for Inspiralized would never have become what it is today. You encouraged me to quit my job and pursue this dream, believing that I could do anything. Your unwavering faith in me brings tears to my eyes and I can't wait to spend the rest of my life with you, making you as happy as you've made me. You not only lift me up but you also keep me there if I ever start to fall. Every single day, I'm inspired and motivated by your own hard work as an entrepreneur, and I couldn't ask for a better person to have along for the ride in this dream journey. Most importantly, thank you for genuinely loving healthy food – you might even love courgette noodles more than I do (doubtful, but maybe!).